# WRITING IN THE CENTER

## TEACHING IN A WRITING CENTER SETTING

*Second Edition*

**Irene L. Clark**
*University of Southern California*

**KENDALL/HUNT PUBLISHING COMPANY**
4050 Westmark Drive Dubuque, Iowa 52002

# CONTENTS

# PREFACE TO THE SECOND EDITION

❖

Writing centers are flourishing. Almost seven years have passed since the first publication of *Writing in the Center*, and during that time, writing centers have attained greater credibility within the academic community and have proliferated across the country, in high schools as well as in colleges and universities. The National Council of Teachers of English and the Conference on College Composition and Communication now regularly hold an exciting array of workshops and panels concerned with writing centers, and meetings of the National Writing Centers Association, once inconspicuous in a corner of a conference room, now require a large hall to house its many regional divisions. Subscriptions to the *Writing Lab Newsletter* continue to grow, and the *Writing Center Journal* has recently celebrated its tenth anniversary. Now, when I mention my profession both within and beyond academic circles, I am less frequently asked "What is a writing center?" and I have learned of the existence of writing centers in Australia, Mexico, and Japan. Happily, as Gary Olson observes, "although writing centers have always been diverse in their pedagogies, philosophies, and physical makeups, the writing center's period of chaotic adolescence is nearly over. Center directors are slowly articulating common goals, objectives, and methodologies, and writing centers are beginning to take on a common form to evolve into a recognizable species" (vii).

Part of this professional credibility can be traced to an increased understanding of the suitability of writing centers for implementing composition theory; in particular, the recent prominence of social constructionist theory and its relationship to a collaborative approach to writing has provided writing centers with a significant theoretical rationale. As the romantic concept of writing as a solitary act has been replaced by the idea of writing as a social process, writing centers are recognized as the appropriate environment for students to receive their first introduction to the academic discourse community. Thus, although writing centers remain eminently practical, flexible, and student oriented, they have moved beyond the realm of the makeshift and the "whatever works" mentality.

Another factor contributing to writing centers' enhanced professional status is the growing recognition that everyone, good writers as well as poor ones, can benefit from visiting a writing center and that even professional writers experience writing block, write multiple revisions, and seek audience feedback. This realization means that writing centers are now less frequently tainted with the stigma of "remediation" with its accompanying overemphasis on mechanical correctness. As a result, the image of the writing center as a dreary place for remedial students to work on "skill and drill" activities has been replaced by a vital one of lively student/tutor interactions and meaningful discoveries.

Validated on both a theoretical and pedagogical level, writing centers have thus achieved new status, and accordingly, this second edition addresses recent theoretical connections as well as provides additional practical suggestions and resources. Essentially, I have not changed the pedagogical precepts I advocated in the first edition, although this edition develops stronger links to rhetorical theory, provides updated examples and dialogues, and additional strategies and models. However, although my view of writing centers has not changed significantly, I have discovered that the act of rewriting resulted in many unanticipated changes. Although I had originally planned to retain the chapter divisions and titles of the first edition, I found that the addition of new content resulted in a redistribution of ideas which, then, created the need for restructuring the chapter divisions and resulted in different chapter titles. The new edition also contains two new chapters, a chapter concerned with the increasingly important topic of computers in the writing center, and a chapter addressing two special assignments, the paper utilizing outside sources and the paper focusing on literature. In addition, the chapter concerned with working with non-native speakers now includes suggestions for working with dialect speakers, and I have included a "Writing Center Resources" section to provide suggestions for further research.

Aside from adding and restructuring, though, I have tried to preserve the aim and spirit of the first edition—that is, I continue to view *Writing in the Center* as a work for new writing center tutors who want to understand what tutoring writing is about and as a resource that writing center directors can use for training and guidance. Most importantly, I hope that this second edition conveys my continued enthusiasm for the work I do and my firm belief that writing centers provide the liveliest, as well as the most effective, arena for helping students learn to write.

# INTRODUCTION

❖

Writing centers are proliferating all over the country—lively, energetic places—and this is a book for those who work in them. Some of us are called "tutors"—some have other titles such as "writing consultants" or "assistants." Whatever we may be called, those of us who work in writing centers play a fundamental role in helping students of all levels learn to write.

Over the past twenty-five years, teaching writing in a writing center has become as important as teaching in a traditional classroom. It is now acknowledged that teaching students to write does not involve lecturing or assigning "how-to" books; instead, we now know what writers have always known—that one learns to write by *writing, talking* about writing, getting *feedback* on one's writing, and then rewriting and rewriting, preferably in a comfortable non-threatening setting. This process is especially well-suited to the flexible environment of the writing center.

Until fairly recently, most tutors and teachers involved in writing centers were given very little preparation or training. Somehow it was assumed that once a potential tutoring staff became conversant with a bit of rhetorical theory and provided with the names of a few reputable textbooks, that it would somehow "sense" the best method of conducting a conference. Often, new tutors were merely given a brief lecture on the necessity of conferencing and then simply thrust into a conference session. Learning to tutor took place, presumably, on the job.

However, increased attention to the role of writing centers in the teaching of composition has brought the realization that learning to be a good tutor requires a self-examination and professional training beyond that which had been customarily provided. We now know that successful writing conferences do not simply "happen" (at least not usually). Most often, they occur because tutors have become experts in the field—they plan their tutoring time, determine a sequence of instruction based on a theoretically grounded diagnosis, and then focus the conference toward the accomplishment of specific goals.

If you are about to become involved in composition tutoring, either in a writing center or as part of a teacher preparation class, then perhaps you may be feeling a bit anxious about your prospective new role. Some of you may envision that first conference session with a certain amount of trepidation. You may wonder how you ought to begin, what you should say to students to put them at ease. Should you imitate teachers and tutors you yourself have had acquaintance with in the past? Stuffy old Professor Higgins was successful in teaching Eliza how to speak proper English, but is that the way you, yourself, wish to tutor? Others of you may be concerned that you don't know enough about composition theory or that you are unsure about how to diagnose a student paper. After all, a writing center conference sometimes lasts only about a half hour, perhaps an hour at most. And sometimes the papers students write need a lot more work than you can cover in that amount of time. How will you know which skill to target? How will you insure that students will learn something that they will be able to apply to their next paper?

These are important questions for prospective writing tutors to ask, and the process of asking them constitutes the first step in preparing to tutor effectively. All learning begins with the asking of questions, and now that you have begun to formulate the questions, you can begin to speculate about the answers.

This book is designed to stimulate both the asking of questions and discovery of at least some of the answers, and I believe that once you have read it, that you will be able to begin tutoring with greater understanding and less anxiety. I think that you will find writing centers interesting and rewarding places to work, as each student is an individual, each paper contains its own strengths and weaknesses, and every conference is a new challenge. And unlike teaching writing in a traditional classroom, tutoring in a writing center frees both students and tutors from the pressure of grades. Both are free to experiment with a variety of approaches and styles.

Of course, tutoring, like teaching or painting or performing, is an art as well as a profession, and some of you are going to feel naturally more comfortable in the tutorial role and to be intuitively better tutors than others. Moreover, becoming an effective tutor is a function of experience and practice, and no amount of reading about tutoring can substitute for spending many hours actually tutoring students in composition and evaluating the quality of that tutoring. A book, though, can generate ideas about a process before that process is actually begun. You have now begun the process of thinking about tutoring. This is the first step in your preparation.

# Chapter One

# Writing and the Writing Center: Theories and Models

I have been involved with writing centers for more than ten years, and during that time, I have seen writing centers spring up all over the country, although sometimes they have other names, such as writing "labs," writing "rooms," or writing "places." One writing center I visited was enclosed in a large glass building nestled in a redwood forest, where students and tutors conferred with one another in spacious, well-lit study spaces. Another, the more usual model, was housed in a converted, under-sized classroom, furnished with only a battered table and a shabby sofa. Whatever their physical characteristics, though, writing centers are now recognized as playing a vital role in the teaching of writing, one that is as pedagogically important as that of the composition classroom.

This chapter discusses why and how writing centers have become so prominent in the field of composition and summarizes several theories and models which pertain to the composing process. Although initially, writing center tutors worry less about theory than they do about practical, day to day strategies (they are concerned primarily about what to say and do and about how to avoid looking like a fool), they soon realize that their tutoring will be more effective if it is based on a coherently thought out concept of how students learn to write. If tutors are not acquainted with theories of writing and learning, they will simply be **guessing** about what is likely to be effective when they work with students in the writing center. An important idea behind this book is that although writing centers address practical concerns, what happens in writing centers is based on a firm theoretical foundation.

Having said this, however, I will introduce the writing center approach with a practical illustration, embodied in the following two scenarios:

### Scenario #1

You are a novice skier, and suddenly you find yourself riding a chairlift, heading inexorably up a steep snowy slope. All alone, close to panicking, you feel the chair climb higher and higher. Suddenly, the top of the slope is upon you, and you slide off, as best you can, fear in your throat, tumbling about until you gain your balance. Upright once again, you attempt to get down the hill as best you can, stumbling over your skis, losing control, standing for hours paralyzed by fear. When you finally do get to the bottom of the slope, you are cold, frightened, and bruised. You have only a vague idea of how you managed to get down and are absolutely terrified of trying again.

### Scenario #2

You are a novice skier, but as you move up the snowy slope, a supportive and well-trained instructor is with you to provide instruction and assistance, one step at a time. The instructor accompanies you on the chairlift and calms your fears as you push off and begin moving down the slope. As you complete each manoeuvre, you receive feedback on what you did properly and advice about how to improve. Once you get down the slope, you feel encouraged to try again, knowing you can always ask for help if you need it. You haven't only gotten to the bottom of the slope; you have also become a better skier!

These two scenarios depict the approach to writing on which the concept of a writing center is based—that is, one can learn to ski or to write by stumbling around, making mistakes and getting hurt, but the learning will be neither efficient nor pleasant. A better way to learn is under benevolent and informed guidance, receiving feedback as needed. Writing centers provide this sort of guidance, and they are important because they effectively facilitate student learning. They do not simply provide a "quick-fix" for flawed student papers; instead, they are centers for individualized writing instruction, enabling students at all levels to become better writers.

# What Is a Writing Center?

Broadly defined, a Writing Center is a facility where writers of all kinds, from a first semester freshman to a faculty member, can come for an individualized writing conference with a knowledgeable, well-trained tutor (I will use the word "tutor" throughout this book, although sometimes they have many other titles, such as "writing consultants," "writing advisors," or "writing assistants"). Writing center tutors work with papers at all stages of the writing process—those that are just in the process of being formulated, as well as rough drafts, or relatively polished efforts which need only slight additional editing. Frequently, students come to the writing center to discuss a writing topic before they have written anything at all, or they may come in with outlines or rough drafts. Talking about writing and working with drafts in progress are considered the most useful writing center activities, although some students also work with writing center materials such as books, handouts on various facets of the writing process, tape recorders or computers.

# How Did Writing Centers Develop?

The two scenarios presented above illustrate the effectiveness of the writing center approach to the teaching of writing. One might ask, though, how writing centers and labs have achieved such pedagogical prominence, when not too long ago they were virtually unknown. After all, writers have been writing throughout the centuries, yet writing centers and labs have been around for only a short time. Why is there now a need for writing centers when it seems that people were once taught to write perfectly well without them?

Of course, one might respond that there are many approaches and techniques currently being used in education that did not exist in the past—computers, tape recorders, and films, to cite only a few examples. The obvious explanation is to point out that writing centers exist simply because they are pedagogically effective—most students find that Writing Centers not only help them write better papers but also to become better **writers** (North 438). The historical explanation, however, is that Writing Centers came into existence in response to an educational crisis generated by a rapid increase in student enrollment about twenty-five years ago, an increase that resulted in many underprepared students attending colleges. Until fairly recently, only a small percentage of the general population participated in any form of higher education, and most of these who did already knew something about writing, because they passionately loved to read and had long been fascinated with the written word. Many of these students seemed to have an intuitive ear for prose and experienced relatively little difficulty generating ideas or developing structure. For these students, writing was a means of self-fulfillment, perhaps a pleasure, and those who aspired to higher education were, by definition, those who already could write. Those who could not were deemed ill-suited for higher education, and little attempt was made to "teach" them.

Over the past twenty-five years, though, students with a wide variety of educational backgrounds and interests began attending colleges and universities. Products of their culture, these students were familiar with the media and relatively articulate; however, many had done little reading and virtually no writing, in school or elsewhere, and were terribly anxious at the thought of having to write the papers required in their college classes. And the papers they wrote made their instructors anxious as well!

After a few years of confusion and speculation about the "decline in standards" and the need to reestablish what was termed the "basics," the needs of this new group of students generated academic interest in how one "learns" to write and in how writing can best be "taught." At first, perhaps because of an underlying cultural conviction that writing is a mysterious process, a virtually unteachable "natural" talent, teachers of writing did not attempt to deal with anything that occurred between the conception of an idea and the completion of a first draft. Teaching writing meant simply the teaching of editing skills: grammar, punctuation, and usage. Students were assigned a topic and went home and wrote their papers, which they then submitted to the instructor for evaluation. The instructor marked the paper up in red, occasionally wrote scathing comments, and assigned grades. Such was the teaching of composition—tedious for instructors, terrifying for students.

Fortunately, though, things have changed. There is now an increased scholarly interest in how writing skills are acquired and how best to teach university level writing. The writing center concept emerged from this interest, as well as from the pragmatic needs of the new student population, and the teaching of writing has undergone a shift in focus from the composed product to the composing process. This theoretical reorientation has correspondingly led to a concern with developing pedagogical strategies for intervening in the writing process at all stages, sometimes before the student has written anything at all or developed even the glimmer of an idea. This type of instruction is particularly well-suited to the flexible structure of writing centers, where instruction is individualized and where students can obtain help with their writing at any stage in the composing process. Writing centers, then, are particularly appropriate for the new composition pedagogy. Students find them comfortable, non-threatening places for learning; teachers find them a satisfying setting for teaching. As Steve North says, the concept of a writing center

> represents the marriage of what are arguably the two most powerful contemporary perspectives on teaching writing: first, that writing is most usefully viewed as a process; and second, that writing curricula need to be student-centered. This new writing center, then, defines its province not in terms of some curriculum, but in terms of the writers it serves (438).

## Writing Centers and Language Development

The concept of the writing center is also consistent with what linguists and psychologists have discovered about language development. Jean Piaget, studying the stages of learning through which children pass from birth to late adolescence, points out that the young child begins perceiving the world totally from his own perspective—that is, his vision is egocentric and his attempts to communicate are through "egocentric speech," whereby he "talks for himself," although he "thinks he is talking for others and is making himself understood" (Piaget 8). A young child, for example, introduced to a stranger, might be discussing something about which the stranger could have no previous information. The child might say, " I fixed the car all by myself," without explaining what car, what wheel, or the problem it had in the first place.

Building upon Piaget's work, L.S. Vygotsky points out that egocentric speech evolves eventually into "inner speech," a mature process of thought, a dynamic "fluttering between word and thought" (*Thought and Language* 249). Written language is perceived by Vygotsky as developed inner speech, "whose predication and condensation give way in writing to fully developed syntax and word specificity" (Foster 13). Vygotsky maintains that the composing process "reflects the process by which inner speech becomes external speech. In the process of communication, reflection in language (inner speech) becomes communication through language (external speech)" (Foster 13).

This concept of stages in writing growth is well suited to writing center teaching, where teachers and tutors can work individually with students at whatever level in their writing abilities they happen to be. The writing center environment also enables students to receive immediate audience feedback on their work, feedback that enables them to become aware of when they are writing "ego-centrically" or, as Linda Flower terms it "writer-based prose," defined as an "unretouched and underprocessed version" (Flower, "Writer-Based Prose" 1979) of the writer's own thought. Writing centers, then, enable teachers of writing to apply what psychological and linguistic theory has discovered about the writing process.

## Writing Centers and Learning

Writing centers additionally utilize the insights gained from theories of learning, since the effectiveness of tutoring is unfluenced by the conditions in which it occurs. According to Jerome Bruner, a well-known learning theorist, students learn best when they are active participants in the learning process, not passive recipients of information. According to Bruner, "to instruct someone in [a] discipline is not a matter of getting him to commit results to mind. Rather it is to teach him to participate in the process that makes possible the establishment of knowledge . . . Knowledge is a process, not a product" (72). Bruner points out that all learning must be viewed as

> a provisional state that has as its object to make the learner or problem solver self-sufficient. Any regimen of correction carries the danger that the learner may become permanently dependent on the tutor's correction. The tutor must direct his instruction in a fashion that eventually makes it possible for the student to take over the corrective function himself. Otherwise, the result of instruction is to create a form of mastery that is contingent upon the perpetual presence of the tutor (53).

Comb and Snygg similarly maintain that a student who learns by discovery is more likely to acquire a sense of adequacy. They feel that too much exposure to lectures, texts, or programs tend to make a student dependent on others and minimizes the likelihood of his seeking answers or solving problems on his own.

The idea of learning by discovery is also consistent with *attribution theory*, a learning theory maintaining that the allocation of responsibility (that is, the particular reason to which one attributes the cause of an event or accomplishment) manifestly guides subsequent behavior. Attribution theory contends that "within achievement related contexts" (Weiner 185), affect is maximized when success and failure are attributed to the internal element of ability and effort, rather than to the external element of luck or change, and that "causal attributions influence the likelihood of undertaking achievement activities, the intensity of work at these activities, and the degree of persistence in the face of failure" (Weiner 195). Thus, according to this theory, in order for students to improve in their writing, they must attribute their success to their own efforts and abilities, not to the skill of the tutor. Thus, writing center ideology stresses the importance of encouraging students to be active participants in their conferences, not disciples sitting in humility at the feet of a mentor.

# Approaches to Composition: Theories and Models

In addition to incorporating theories of learning and language acquisition, writing centers implement several approaches to the teaching of writing developed from recent scholarly interest in composition. These approaches may be defined according to which element in the act of writing they emphasize: the writer, the prospective reader, or the community or context. Of course, when writing occurs, all of these elements impact one another, functioning interdependently; however, for instructional purposes, each can be examined separately. In this section, I shall focus on three principal approaches to composition pedagogy: **process theory, reading theory,** and **social constructionist theory.**

## The Process Approach

The process approach to composition emphasizes the **writer;** it is concerned primarily with the activities writers engage in when they create and produce a text. This approach evolved as a reaction to the dominance of a product-centered pedagogy that focused on error correction and formulaic patterns of organization. In contrast, the process approach is concerned with **how** writers produce texts and with helping writers develop an effective writing process.

The concept of viewing writing as a process became prominent through the early work of Wallas and the later refinements of Winterowd, and of Young, Becker, and Pike. Their work resulted in a model based on several overlapping and recursive stages: starting point, exploration, incubation, illumination, composing, reformulation, and editing. The starting point is the point at which the writing task is perceived as a problem to be solved. The *exploration* stage includes all the preparatory work—collecting data, doing research, brainstorming for relevant memories and experiences, focusing on the problem to be solved. During *incubation,* the conscious mind withdraws from concentration on the problem, so that the subconscious mind may take over. "Creative figures in many disciplines have attested to the necessity of this conscious withdrawal—and withdrawal from consciousness—from the task at hand in order to free our less understood creative forces" (Freedman 4). The *illumination* is the moment when our ideas take shape. What had been a formless mass of information is now focused on a particular purpose.

*Composing* takes place either before, during, and after the moment of illumination. Reformulation involves the reworking of the thesis in terms of language and meaning. Editing involves ore technical matters of mechanics, punctuation, and spelling, or, as Winterowd writes, "the adjustment of the 'surface' of the text so that it approximates . . . Edited Standard English" (163).

Emig, having observed the composing process of twelfth graders, similarly describes the writing process as consisting of prewriting, planning, starting, and reformulating. Britton, Burgess, MacLeod, and Martin emphasized three elements in the writing process: *conception,* which ends when the writer knows he is going to write and has some idea of what is expected of him, *incubation,* and finally *production.* Britton and his colleagues say, too, that when a writer takes on a task as soon as it is set, the three elements are likely to be concurrent.

In all of these process oriented models, words such as "prewriting," "writing," and "rewriting" may suggest that writing is a linear process that can be divided into distinct sequential steps. However, research in composition suggests that the writing process is *recursive,* that is, cyclical and fluid, rather than linear and stage-bound (USC Freshman Writing Orientation Notebook). As the writing process model presented here indicates, most writers shift back and forth in composing and may use all elements of the process at different moments, maybe at the same time. As Graser describes it,

> Think of three separate metal rings, interlocked, each able to move in its own plane, but not separable. As you twirl one ring backward and forward, for the moment you let the other two slip out of your attention; yet moving one ring, you may reveal a previously unseen aspect of the others. You know that moving one will cause the others to move, but you look at each separately for a clearer view. We may name one *prewriting,* another *writing,* and the third *rewriting.* We can look at them one at a time, but we can't separate them. Writers may be concerned with any or all of them in any sequence (5).

Concerned with avoiding models that suggest that the writing process is linear, Flower and Hayes set up a cognitive theory based on four points:

1. The process of writing is best understood as a set of distinctive think processes that writers orchestrate or organize during the act of composing.

2. These processes have a hierarchical highly embedded organization in which any process can be embedded within any other.

3. The act of composing itself is a goal-directed thinking process, guided by the writers' own growing network of goals.

4. Writers create their own goals in two key ways: by generating both high-level goals and supporting sub-goals that embody the writer's developing sense of purpose, and then, at times, by changing major goals or even establishing new ones based on what has been learned in the act of writing (Flower and Hayes 366).

### *The Process Approach and the Writing Center*

The writing center provides an ideal setting for implementing the process approach to the teaching of writing. In the writing center, tutors can work with students throughout the composing process, changing and rearranging goals and subgoals. As they discover new directions for their texts, students can return to invention strategies even after they have written a first draft, engaging in additional brainstorming and developing additional material. Thus, the process approach in the writing center enables students to learn experimentally that writing is a process of rethinking, and that writing means rewriting.

The writing center also implements process by providing opportunities for students to practice different kinds of writing strategies. They can work with invention, planning, organization, and revision strategies that will not only improve the paper they are working on, but can also be applied to a subsequent writing task.

## Reading Theory and the Writer-Reader Transaction

While process theory emphasizes the writer, reading theory, emphasizes the *reader*, in particular, the relationship between the writer and the reader, the text serving as the means of creating a dialogue between the two. Reading theory envisions the writer as a person engaged in a dialogue with an audience, a dialogue impacted by the role of world knowledge and the reader's expectations. Recent reading theorists, such Kenneth Goodman or Frank Smith, "conceive of reading not as the passive decoding of information but as the active construction of meaning by a reader within a cultural and cognitive context" (USC Freshman Writing Orientation Notebook).

Reading theory points out that readers bring world knowledge to a text; that is, they bring a great deal more information than the text itself supplies, and that information affects how that text will be understood or interpreted. A successful writer, then, must consider what sort of knowledge the reader is likely to bring to the text, and to provide background material, when necessary.

The role of knowledge and reader expectation in the creation of a text is embodied in two terms coined by Linda Flower: *writer-based prose* and *reader-based prose*. Writer-based prose, like Vygotsky's egocentric speech discussed above, refers to prose that only the writer can understand, because he or she has not adequately considered the needs of the reader. Writer-based prose is associated with early drafts of a text, in which the writer is simply throwing out ideas, without providing adequate "cueing" or signalling devices to aid the reader. Through revision, however, the writer can convert writer-based prose into reader-based prose, that is, writing that provides adequate background information and cueing strategies, so that the text can be understood by a reader.

This idea that a writer engages in a dialogue with the reader supports the importance of talking through a paper before beginning to write. Britton points out that "the relationship of talk to writing is central to the writing process" (29) in that talk permits "the expression of tentative conclusions and opinions . . . The free flow of talk allows ideas to be bandied about, and opens up new relationships, so that explaining the whole thing to oneself may be much easier" (30).

### The Reader-Writer Transaction and the Writing Center

Writing centers are extremely well-suited for clarifying the transaction between the reader and the writer, since by assuming a non-evaluative, non-threatening role, writing center tutors can act as receptive readers. Connections between reader and writer are easily established in the writing center, because the writing center tutor responds not in the form of written comments in margins, a technique that reinforces distance between reader and writer, but rather in the form of questions, which call for immediate student response. When a tutor indicates that he or she has misread the text or is lacking some important information, students easily understand the necessity of including the necessary information or textual clues and can easily provide them on the spot.

Viewing text in terms of the reader-writer transaction provides an important foundation for writing centers, in that talking is a vital component of the writing center approach. Talking through a paper enables students to probe further into their topics, conversational banter often leading to serious exploration and discovery.

## Social Constructionism and the Discourse Community

Writing process theory emphasizes the *writer*. Reading theory emphasizes the *reader* and the interaction of the writer with the reader. Social constructionist theory emphasizes the importance of the *context* or *community* for which the text is being written. The principle idea of social constructionist theory is that all knowledge is social knowledge, derived from our surroundings. According to Bakhtin, language

> lies on the borderline between oneself and the other. The word in language is half someone else's. It becomes 'one's own' only when the speaker populates it with his own intentions, his own accent, when he appropriates the word, adapting it to his own semantic and expressive intention. Prior to this moment of appropriation, the word does not exist in a neutral and personal language . . . but rather it exists in other people's mouths, in other people's contexts, serving other people's intentions; it is from there that one must take the word and make it one's own (cited in Ede).

The current research of Marilyn Cooper, Ann Gere, Patricia Bizzell, and Kenneth Bruffee is concerned with viewing writing as "an activity through which a person is continually engaged with a variety of socially constructed systems" (Cooper 36).

An important idea in social constructionist theory is the term "discourse community," which may be defined as a community of knowledgeable peers who share common assumptions, goals, methods of communication, and conventions. According to this definition, an important function of education is to help students become an accepted member of an academic discourse community.

## Social Constructionism and the Writing Center

In her essay "Writing as a Social Process: A Theoretical Foundation for Writing Centers?" Lisa Ede points out the relevance of social constructionist theory for the collaborative approach to writing characteristic of writing centers. Citing the work of Hawkins, Bruffee, and others, Ede emphasizes the importance of replacing the deeply ingrained romantic concept of writing as a solitary individual act with the idea of viewing writing as a social process, a view that involves collaboration and recognizes the importance of context. Ede stresses that this view of writing is vital to establishing the centrality of what occurs in writing centers and she calls for those who work in writing centers to "do case studies, or even more detailed ethnographic analyses" (11) to gain a better understanding of collaborative learning.

Social constructionist theory becomes particularly relevant to writing center teaching in terms of helping students learn the conventions of the academic discourse community. Student essays are often flawed because students do not understand what is meant by an academic argument or how to support their arguments plausibly—in the writing center, tutors can focus on helping students become aware of these conventions. Social constructionist theory also becomes relevant when tutors help students develop a sense of appropriate academic style and tone. This also includes increasing student sensitivity to grammar, spelling, and mechanics, errors which immediately label the student as an outsider to the academic discourse community and consequently can seriously impede the effectiveness of the text.

These three approaches to composition, writing process theory, reading theory, and social constructionist theory provide a theoretical basis for the important teaching and learning that goes on in writing centers. Becoming aware of these theories, and developing strategies deriving from them will help you work in the writing center more effectively.

## Recent Writing Center Scholarship

This chapter provided a brief overview of several theories and models pertaining to writing and learning and the relationship of these theories to the kind of teaching that occurs in the writing center. Tutors also find it useful to read more recent publications concerned with writing centers, in particular, *The Writing Lab Newsletter* and the *Writing Center Journal*, addresses for which are listed at the end of this chapter, if you wish to subscribe. *The Writing Lab Newsletter* is filled with useful suggestions and discussions of practical tutoring strategies, while the *Writing Center Journal* focuses on more theoretical concerns. Both of these publications will enable you to approach tutoring with greater insight.

### Applying Theory to Practice

Jason has come to the writing center with the following paper. In small groups, discuss what you feel are the strengths and weaknesses of the paper and the sort of revisions you would suggest for Jason. Then write a paper discussing how you would apply process theory, reading theory, and social constructionist theory in working with him.

_____ **Writing Topic** _____

*There is no question that the electronic media—T.V., radio, movies—have profoundly influenced society in the twentieth century. The media have been seen as factors in everything from the creation of designer jeans to the election of the American president. Because of their influence, the electronic media have generated a great deal of debate regarding their potential for both good and evil.*

*In a well-written essay, address the following question:*

### Has the Influence of the Electronic Media Been Harmful to Society? Why or Why Not?

*In your response, you should focus on specific ways the media have influenced society. You may wish to consider one or two of the following issues: myths and illusions created by the media, racial and sexual stereotypes, consumerism, social values, political values, the depiction of crime and violence. However, you are not limited to these choices and are encouraged to select your own.*

─────────────────── **Student Essay** ───────────────────

Television sets are on in millions of homes across the United States an average of 12 hours a day. Television has become the major source of information. After all, why read when you can sit back, relax, and watch television. Americans receive information about everything from world affairs to problems in America alone to what is happening in their community. The problem is, though, that the electronic media has tended to promote stereotypes, especially about families, minorities, and sexual values. Thus, I would say that the electronic media has harmed rather than helped society.

Television has created the illusion that the nuclear family is alive and well. Situation comedies such as The Cosby Show, Family Ties, and Growing Pains portray a happy nuclear family. Every week problems are overcome. In one episode of Growing Pains, Mike, the son, is offered drugs. He, of course, refuses and all is well as his parents praise him and tell him how proud they are of him because he did not give in to peer pressure. However, in reality, peer pressure is very strong. However, this is not the only illusion. The nuclear family is not alive because families are no longer together since half of all marriages end up in divorce. The nuclear family is not the exception rather than the rule.

All kinds of racial stereotypes are enforced by the electronic media. Japanese are shown as having oily, stringy, black hair, wearing glasses, and speaking funny. Gung Ho, a situation comedy, does exactly this. Gung Ho is about a Japanese company taking over a dead American automobile factory. And every week the Japanese are ridiculed and made fun of as the smart Caucasians play tricks. Blacks and Hispanics are perceived to have no education, no jobs and supposed to live a life of crime. In detective shows such as Spencer, the main character who is white helps fight crime every week. He puts countless numbers of blacks in jail. Whites are shown almost always in white collar jobs. In LA Law, every one is Caucasian. In 227, the black father is a construction worker. Homosexuals are also shown as people apart from the human race. In Three's Company, Jack pretends to be gay in order to live with his two female roommates. So, in front of the manager he always acts feminine.

Commercials on the television also send messages to young girls that they must be beautiful, thin, and have a great body. The California girl is in. Pringles potato chips has beautiful girls lying by the pool eating their product. The guys must also be good looking but to a lesser degree. What men have to be is rich in order to get the girl.

Unless the electronic media changes its programming drastically, all of these stereotypes will continue to be seen by countless viewers. Television affects the way we perceive different things and so far it has not done an accurate job.

## Assessing Your Own Process

Think about papers you have written for classes, and write an essay describing your own writing process. Include in your discussion an analysis of how process, reading, and social constructionist theory could help you understand your own process.

## For Further Exploration

In addition to the works cited at the end of this chapter, you can use the following suggestions to initiate further inquiry into the complex subject of writing pedagogy. An excellent source for investigating theories and ideas that impact the writing center is *The Bedford Bibliography for Teachers of Writing. 3rd edition.* edited by Patricia Bizzell and Bruce Herzberg. New York: Bedford Books of St. Martin's Press, 1991.

### Writing Process Theory

Britton, James et al. *The Development of Writing Abilities (11–18)* London: Macmillan Education Ltd, 1975.

Elbow, Peter. *Embracing Contraries: Explorations in Learning and Teaching.* New York: Oxford University Press, 1986.

Emig, Janet. *The Composing Processes of Twelfth Graders.* Urbana, Illinois: NCTE, 1971.
   *The Web of Meaning: Essays on Writing: Teaching, Learning, and Thinking.* Montclair, New Jersey: Boynton/Cook, 1983.

Flower, Linda S. "The Construction of Purpose in Writing and Reading." *College English* 50 (September 1988): 528–50.

Graser, Elsa. *Teaching Writing: A Process Approach.* Dubuque, Iowa: Kendall/Hunt Publishing Company, 1983.

Harris, Muriel, and Katherine E. Rowan. "Explaining Grammatical Concepts." Journal of Basic Writing, 6 (Fall 1989): 21–41.

Kroll, Barry M. and Hohn Schafer. "Error Analysis and the Teaching of Composition." *College Composition and Communication.* 29 (October 1978): 242–248.

Lindemann, Erika. *A Rhetoric For Writing Teachers.* New York: Oxford University Press, 1982.

Sommers, Nancy. Revision Strategies of Student Writers and Experienced Adult Writers." *College Composition and Communication.* 31 (December 1980): 378–388.

Winterowd, W. Ross. "Developing a Composition Program." *Reinventing the Rhetorical Tradition.* Ed Aviva Freedman and Ian Pringle. Conway Arkansas: L&S Books, 1980.

Young, Richard E., Alton L. Becker, and Kenneth L. Pike. *Rhetoric: Discovery and Change.* New York: Harcourt, 1970.

### Reading Theory

Dillon, George L. *Constructing Texts: Elements of a Theory of Composition and Style.* Bloomington, Indiana: Indiana University Press, 1981.

Gibson, Eleanor J. and Harry Levin. *The Psychology of Reading.* Cambridge, Mass.: MIT Press, 1980.

Goodman, Kenneth S. "A Psycholinguistic Guessing Game." *Journal of the Reading Specialist* 6 (1967): 126–135.

Kirsch, Gesa, and Duane H. Roen. A Sense of Audience in Written Communication. Newbury Park, California: Sage Publications, 1990.

Smith, Frank. *Writing and the Writer.* New York: Holt, Rinehart and Winston, 1982.

### Social Constructionist Theory

Bruffee, Kenneth. "Collaborative Learning and the 'Conversation of Mankind.'" College English 46 (1984): 635–652.

———. "Social Construction, Language, and the Authority of Knowledge: A Bibliographical Essay." *College English* 48 (1986): 773–790.

Cooper, Marilyn M. and Michael Holzman. *Writing as Social Action.* Portsmouth, New Hampshire: Heinemann, Boynton/Cook, 1989.

Ede, Lisa. "Writing as a Social Process: A Theoretical Foundation For Writing Centers." *The Writing Center Journal* 9.2 (1989): 3–15.

Harris, Joseph. "The Idea of Community in the Study of Writing." *College Composition and Communication.* 40 (February 1989): 11–22.

Trimbur, John. "Consensus and Difference in Collaborative Learning." *College English,* 51 (October 1989): 602–616.

## Works Cited

Britton, James et al. *The Development of Writing Abilities* 11–18. London: Macmillan, 1975.

Bruner, Jerome. *Toward a Theory of Instruction.* Cambridge, Mass.: The Belknap Press of Harvard University Press, 1966.

Comb, Arthur C. and Donald Snygg. *Individual Behavior,* revised edition (Harper: New York, 1959).

Cooper, Marilyn. "The Ecology of Writing." *College English* 48 (1986): 364–75.

Ede, Lisa. "Writing as a Social Process: A Theoretical Foundation For Writing Centers." *The Writing Center Journal* 9.2 (1989): 3–15.

Emig, Janet. *The Composing Process of Twelfth Graders. Research Report No. 13.* Urbana: NCTE, 1971.

Flower, Linda. "Writer-Based Prose: A Cognitive Basis for Problems in Writing." *College English* 41 (September 1979): 19–38.

Flower, Linda and John Hayes. "A Cognitive Process Theory of Writing." *College Composition and Communication* 32 (1981): 365–388.

Foster, David. A Primer for Writing Teachers. Upper Montclair, Boynton/Cook, 1983.

Freedman, Aviva. "A Theoretic Context for the Writing Lab." in *Tutoring Writing: A Sourcebook for Writing Labs,* ed. Muriel Harris. Glenview, Illinois: Scott Foresman, 1982.

Graser, Elsa. *Teaching Writing: A Process Approach.* Dubuque, Iowa: Kendall/Hunt,1983.

North, Stephen. "The Idea of a Writing Center." *College English* 46 (1984): 443–447.

Piaget, Jean. *The Language and Thought of the Child.* New York: New American Library, 1974.

Vygotsky, Lev S. *Thought and Language.* trans Eugenia Hanfmann and Gertrude Vakar. Cambridge, Mass.: MIT Press, 1962.

Weiner, Bernard. *Achievement Motivation and Attribution Theory.* New Jersey: General Learning Press, 1974.

Winterowd, W. Ross. "Developing a Composition Program." *Reinventing the Rhetorical Tradition.* ed. Aviva Freedman and Ian Pringle. Conway, Arkansas: L&S Books, 1980.

# Chapter Two

# Anticipating Tutoring: Remembering, Reflecting, Imagining

You can prepare for an exam by studying the material to be covered. You can prepare to run a marathon by running every day and building up your stamina. In fact, preparation for almost any type of performance—acting, singing, juggling—can be achieved through rigorous practice. But if you have never taught or tutored before, what can you do to prepare yourself for tutoring in a writing center? This chapter raises several issues that will enable you to *anticipate* tutoring. You will be asked to reflect on what you already know and believe about writing, to remember your own experience as a student writer, and to imagine possible interactions with student writers. My feeling is that anticipating tutoring is a good way to prepare for working in a writing center, so that when you actually begin to tutor, you will be more confident and effective.

## Reflecting on Your Own Writing Process

A first and obvious recommendation for anyone who plans to work with writers, whether in a writing center or in a classroom, is to write a great deal yourself and become aware of how you do it. Anyone who teaches writing ought to be a writer—of papers, reports, letters, journals, diaries, notes—engaging in any kind of writing can help you learn about the writing process. The important thing is to write often (possibly every day), observe yourself as you write, and gain insight into your own composing process. How do you generate ideas for a paper? Do you cluster or brainstorm before you write? Do you always know what you plan to say before you sit down to write? Or does your main idea emerge from a haphazardly scribbled, possibly unfocused first draft? Do you sketch an outline for yourself before you write? Or does your organizational structure become apparent to you only after you have been writing? Do you write in stages? Or do you tackle the whole essay in one exhausting marathon session? Do you do all or any of these activities on a computer? These are questions you should ask yourself as a way of anticipating tutoring.

## Exercise

Spend thirty minutes writing about how you write papers for your classes. To focus your thinking, consider a particular paper you wrote. Some questions you might consider are as follows:

1. How long did you spend writing the paper?
2. Did you spend time thinking about it before you wrote it? When do you do your thinking?
3. Did you do any research?
4. Did you use any method for generating text? Clustering? Freewriting? Sketchy notes?
5. Did you write an outline?
6. How many drafts did you write?
7. Do you read aloud when you go over your paper? Do you read to someone else?
8. How do you revise and edit your paper? Do you revise substantially or simply "tinker" with the surface? Do you use a computer?
9. Is the setting important to you when you write? Do you sit in a special chair or at a desk or table, for example?

Writing this paper will help you think about your own writing process, insight that may give you some good ideas when you tutor. When you finish writing your paper, break into small groups and read your papers aloud to one another, discussing particular ideas that may or may not be applicable for tutoring.

# Reflecting on Evaluation

Although many of you have never tutored before, you bring to your new role some fairly definite ideas about writing and teaching, ideas that you absorbed when you were a student or that you hold simply because you are a member of the culture. As a tutor you should become aware of these ideas, so that you can decide how well they correspond to your concept of what tutoring can or ought to be. Some of these ideas you may find quite compatible with your ideal; others you may wish to reject. To gain awareness about some of your positions concerning evaluation, take a few minutes to indicate how much you agree with the following statements:

### Ideas on Evaluation

1. The papers students bring to the writing center should be evaluated primarily for content, not for style and structure.
2. Good spelling is important.
3. Neatness is important.
4. Low grades and poor evaluations usually create incentives for students to work harder.
5. Students who are poor writers are usually unintelligent.
6. It is best to give many more positive than negative evaluations.
7. The worth of a piece of writing depends primarily on how successfully it fulfills the assignment.
8. Students should not be encouraged to grade themselves.
9. Some people can write; other people cannot.
10. It is important to consider alternate grading systems to the generally accepted ones.

Each of the statements on this list can provide a topic for discussion. After indicating the extent to which you agree with each of them, break into small groups and discuss your responses. Are there many differences in how each person responds? Is there a particular response which you think is appropriate or inappropriate for effective tutoring? Do your responses vary according to whether or not you are looking at a first draft?

For example, consider your position on spelling, neatness, and mechanical correctness, the reputed concerns of stereotypical teachers. How do you think you react to papers containing multiple errors? Do you tend to think that writers who make such errors are not intelligent, even if the papers containing these errors are first drafts? Or can you overlook these sorts of problems in the interest of other concerns, such as form or content?

Then consider what you believe about motivation and its relationship to grades. Do you, yourself, work more diligently for a hard grader? Or does the threat of a poor grade freeze you into immobility? What do you think about not grading at all?

Now think about what you believe about writing ability. Do you have a secret belief that there are some gifted people who write by inspiration, the romantic myth of our culture? Do you perhaps think that students who can't write properly do not belong in college? Or do you believe that writing is a skill that almost anyone can master if he or she is willing to work hard? Which of these ideas are best suited for working in a writing center?

These are important questions to ask yourself in thinking about tutoring, because even though writing centers are not really in the "evaluation business," and, in fact, make concerted attempts to avoid direct evaluation, tutors may inadvertently give implicit evaluative messages to students that can jeopardize the effectiveness of their tutoring. If you are aware of your position on evaluation, you will be able to exercise some control over the kinds of comments you give to students when you tutor. Directly stated critical comments such as "this paper isn't good because . . ." or "You haven't answered the question. This paper is way off topic" tend to intimidate students without helping them understand what they should do to improve their writing. Tutoring in a writing center means **enabling** students to make their own evaluations and to work with students to develop strategies for improvement.

## Reflecting on Collaboration

Writing center pedagogy advocates a **collaborative** relationship between tutor and student—that is, the tutor and the student work together, so that the student gains insight into his or her own writing process while improving the text under discussion. A collaborative relationship means that the tutor does not "take charge" of either the conference or the text, since students learn best when they discover methods and ideas for themselves and are active participants in the learning process.

However, as much as one might believe in the value of collaborative learning, it is not always easy to achieve. John Trimbur points out that tutoring in a writing center setting requires "a balancing act that asks tutors to juggle roles, to shift identity, to know when to act like an expert and when to act like a co-learner." (25). This sort of balance can be difficult to maintain, not only because students often pressure for more directive assistance (students want their grades to improve. They are less concerned with long term writing improvement) but also because most of us, in our own school experience, have had little exposure to this sort of learning and have few good models to imitate.

I'LL WRITE
A CONCLUSION
NEXT TIME,
**I PROMISE!**

DEALING WITH ASSERTIVENESS

What also makes it difficult to achieve collaboration in the writing center is that our culture does not usually conceive of writing as a collaborative activity, and therefore, collaboration in any form is regarded with a certain amount of suspicion. In a conference presentation a few years ago, Karen Hodges discussed the wide diversity in attitude toward collaborative effort among various disciplines, concluding that English Departments, unlike departments in the natural and social sciences, tend to focus heavily on style, and thus, ironically, were least likely to favor collaboration between student and tutor (see Clark 1988). In the humanities, in particular, writing a paper, as opposed to studying for an exam, has historically been viewed as an individual act. Referring to his own participation in study groups as an undergraduate, Trimbur states, "If Western Civilization was seen as a collective problem, permitting a collective response, writing was apparently an individual problem, private and displaced from the informal network of mutual aid" (2). Bruffee, too, points out that "collaboration and community activity is inappropriate and foreign to work in humanistic disciplines, such as English. Humanistic study, we have been led to believe, is a solitary act" (645). Since writing center tutors often come from an English department or humanities background, they are often completely unfamiliar with the idea of collaborative learning.

The other point to reflect on when you think about collaborative writing is to consider the difference between **legitimate** and **illegitimate** collaboration. One point to consider is that true collaboration, in its pure form, can occur only when collaborators are part of the same discourse community and meet as equals. True colleagues regularly communicate by discussing each other's work, assisting one another by suggesting sources, trading drafts, or perhaps suggesting stylistic changes. This type of what could be referred to as "collegial" collaboration is motivated by the desire to offer additional perspectives that can be helpful even to competent writers, and the collaboration may be considered "legitimate" in that there is mutual respect between participants. It assumes that the author, not the collaborator will be ultimately responsible for the evolving text (see Clark 1990). For example, I have a colleague, to whom I might show a draft of a work in progress, and she might indeed make some suggestions for revision. But she would not attempt to completely rewrite my text and the text would ultimately still reflect my ideas, my style, and my purpose.

Illegitimate collaboration, in contrast, occurs when the tutor provides so much input into the student's text that the text reflects as much of the tutor's insights as it does of the student's. The tutor has "taken over" the text to such an extent that it achieves a quality that the student would be incapable of attaining on her own. Aside from the ethics involved from this sort of collaboration, when the tutor assumes too much control over either the conference or the paper, the student doesn't learn very much, although he or she may be happy with the improved grade. But since the tutor has done the work, the student will be in no better position to write the next paper.

Whenever I talk to new tutors about the importance of making sure that students do their own work, I like to illustrate it with the story of an experience I recently had with my vacuum cleaner. Not too long ago, I was faced with the puzzling task of changing the bag on a vacuum cleaner that was relatively new, so that I had never changed the bag before. Since my husband was out of town, I decided to tackle the task on my own (had he been in town, I must confess that I probably would not have even attempted to change the bag). However, since mechanical tasks are not my strong suit, I had a great deal of difficulty fitting the bag so that it wouldn't blow off as soon as I started the vacuum cleaner. I tried really hard, reading and rereading the directions, trying to get it right. But finally, when I seemed to be making no progress, I did what any liberated woman would do—I called the man next door, who came over and quickly changed the bag for me.

The point of this story is that because the man next door did it for me, I still do not know how to put a new bag on the vacuum cleaner and would encounter the same problem the next time it needed changing. However, had he *shown* me how to do it or *directed* me to do it myself, I might then have learned. Similarly, when students come to the writing center, tutors should not take over the writing task for them, or else the student will not learn anything that can be applied to a subsequent writing task.

To prepare for tutoring, then, I suggest that you reflect on your own attitude toward collaborative effort in writing. Do you ever request assistance from a peer, a friend, or a family member when you write papers for your classes? Have you ever participated in a group project in writing? Do you anticipate being more or less directive in your tutoring? Think in advance about your preconceptions of the tutoring scene. If you envision a situation in which the tutor speaks and the student listens (such a model is easy to imagine), then replace it in your mind with one in which the student is doing more of the talking. Creating a model in your mind is a good way to anticipate tutoring.

## Anticipating Tutoring by Remembering How it Feels to Be a Student

Many of you were probably composition students at one time in your lives. For some of you, that time may not have been very long ago; for others, it may have been too long ago to remember very clearly. And some of you may prefer to forget.

It is important to remember this time in your life so that you will be able to deal effectively and insightfully with the students you tutor. So to prepare for tutoring, think back on the days when you were the age of your current students. Picture yourself in a composition classroom—get in touch with the sights, the sounds, the smells—and recall some of the papers you wrote at that time. Did you have difficulty with certain topics? Did you sometimes write papers at the last minute? Did you feel sick inside when you received a poor grade on a paper or when your paper was returned to you all marked up? Did you ever talk with your instructor about your writing?

### Exercise

After thinking about this time in your life, write a short essay in which you recall what it was like for you to be a student writing papers for classes. Be as specific as possible, but don't take a great deal of time to revise. Just write as rapidly as possible. Then break into groups and share what you have written, discussing what you liked and disliked about these experiences. Or, if you do not wish to discuss your own writing at this time, you may prefer to discuss Julie's essay, reproduced below.

──────────── **Student Essay** ────────────

Before I came to college, I had always loved to write. In fact, I was so confident about my writing that I usually said outright that I was a "good" writer. In High School, I wrote for the school newspaper, and on my own, I wrote little poems and stories. Writing for me was not a subject I worried a lot about.

Then, in the second semester of my Freshman year at college, I took a class in what was supposed to be Creative Writing, which consisted of reading and analyzing short stories and then writing short narratives ourselves. The teacher, one of the "masters" in his field, was absolutely obsessed with symbolism in fiction, and once I was in his class I developed the idea that every short story had to have symbols in it in order for it to be considered any good. This worried me a great deal when I was writing, and I would spend hours trying to think of symbolic codes to insert into my own stories. I hardly thought at all about things like plot or character.

What terrified me particularly, though, was the method the teacher used to analyze and evaluate student papers. Often, he would have the students sit on a chair in front of the room and read their papers aloud to the class (I can still see in my mind the blur of faces and hear the quavering echo of my own voice as I read.). Then, in the interest of academic standards, he would simply rip the paper to shreds, metaphorically, I mean, of course. Often he was nasty or condescending, asking rhetorical questions, actually sneering at us. He couldn't believe our ignorance. The rest of the class was too frightened to say very much, so he would always call on someone for a comment, and that person would desperately search around for something—anything—to say.

His written comments were equally destructive to students. Papers were usually returned full of red ink; it seemed at the time that everything I wrote had a circle around it. I recall being particularly surprised and devastated by some of his comments because I had always considered myself a good writer. On one paper I wrote, for example, the professor insisted that I didn't know how to use a comma properly and that I look up the appropriate section in the Harbrace Handbook. Anxious to please, of course I did as he requested, but I never could understand what errors I had made, and was too afraid to ask him.

Curiously enough, I did get something out that class—a great respect of how hard it was to write well, an upgrading of my own standards for good writing, and, of course, an awareness of symbolism. But it was a long time before I was brave enough to sign up for another writing class or before I ever thought of myself as a "good" writer. Actually, I am still not too sure about that.

## Questions for Discussion

1. What particular activities and behaviors that you recall from your own experience in writing classes can you apply when you begin to tutor?
2. What particular activities and behaviors from your past were *not effective* in teaching you how to write?

## Questions Concerning Julie's Paper

1. Julie seems quite negative about her experiences in the Creative Writing class. What are some of the techniques and experiences she mentions that were not helpful in teaching her to write?
2. Did Julie gain anything positive from that class?

*Exercise*

After you have discussed your own essays and perhaps Julie's essay as well, break into groups and formulate a statement of what an ideal tutor should be like. Do you think it will be possible for you to realize your model? Why or why not?

# Anticipating Tutoring by Reflecting and Imagining How You Work with Others

All kinds of things can happen when you tutor (actually, that's what makes it interesting), and, of course, it is impossible to anticipate every student and every possible situation that might occur. However, you can expect that certain types of situations are likely to happen so that you can prepare yourself for them. Such preparation involves becoming aware of how you are likely to react and thinking about effective strategies.

## Dealing with Students from Another Culture

In a writing center, tutors are likely to be working with students from a wide variety of cultures and backgrounds, and many of them will have backgrounds, values, and mannerisms quite different from your own. How will you feel working with these students? Will you be able to transcend cultural stereotypes and prejudices and refrain from judging students before you get to know them?

Moreover, it is sometimes the case that students from other cultures will prejudge you, because they perceive you in terms of a stereotype. As Arkin and Shollar point out:

> If students are members of a racial minority, black or Latin, for example, some of them may be tempted to see you as part of the white power structure from which they are excluded, and by whom they are often judged inferior. In doing this, they are stereotyping you, assuming that because some people in the white culture are racists, you too are a racist. If some tutees feel this way, they will naturally be very resistant to working with you; and you, on the other hand, will probably find it difficult to work with these students. Or, you may be a minority tutor assigned some white tutees who think nonwhites inferior. Because these tutees devalue you, they may feel the tutorial is worthless. (128)

(✱) YOU CALL THIS A TOPIC SENTENCE?

MANY IDEAS ABOUT TEACHING AND
WRITING ARE CULTURAL IN ORIGIN

One way to prepare yourself for working with people from another culture is to become aware of your own preconceptions and prejudices. In preparation for tutoring, then, take a walk around your high school or college campus and notice people who are of another race or culture. How do you feel about these people? Do you have preconceptions about what strengths and weaknesses they might have?

You might record these observations in a journal and share parts of it with fellow tutors. Then, when you are actually tutoring, you might record your reactions to particular students you meet in the writing center. How do you react to these students? How do you think they react to you?

## Dealing with Assertiveness

Another way of anticipating tutoring is to gain awareness of how you deal with assertiveness, both your own and that of students. In some tutorial situations, you may have to act more decisively than you usually do. How comfortable are you with being assertive? Does it make you anxious to have to confront a student? How do you feel, for example, about the following interchange?

**Student:** I didn't have time to rewrite my conclusion and I have to hand the paper in to my teacher next period. Can you please rewrite it for me?

**Tutor:** Alright. I don't like to do this. But just this once.

Obviously, the tutor should have been more assertive in his response to the student? How would you have responded to this student's request?

Now read through another example:

**Tutor:** Have you written a rough draft for the paper?
**Student:** No, I decided to go to the game and I didn't have time.
**Tutor:** Well, you keep telling me that you want at least a "B" in the course. But now the paper is due tomorrow and you don't have a draft yet. I guess you really don't care about the grade.

How do you feel about the tutor's response to the student? Do you feel that he was *too* assertive and might possibly anger the student into not coming back? Or can you conceive of a situation in which students might need some kind of confrontation as a motivator?

## Dealing with Assertiveness Through Writing and Discussion

In a group create a set of difficult situations connected with a writing center setting. Write a portion of a dialogue in which it is necessary for the tutor to be assertive. Then read these aloud and discuss them. Some examples of situations are provided below:

1. The student is persistently late. She arrives at least fifteen minutes after the time of her appointment.
2. The student has been assigned to come to the writing center by her teacher, but she does not think she needs any help.
3. The student has plagiarized material from the textbook.
4. The student does not think that you know what you are talking about.

## Dealing with Assertiveness Through Role Playing

Role playing is an activity in which someone imitates another person's behavior (plays a role) in order to gain awareness, learn a skill, or anticipate problematic situations. Role playing is a helpful activity in preparing for tutoring in that it helps identify problems, generates discussions and feedback, and helps develop self-confidence.

## Exercise

Roleplay some of the situations associated with assertiveness that you iden-
tified above. In small groups, discuss what you have learned.

### Roleplaying Other Situations

Here are some other situations that typically occur in a writing center. Role
play some of them in small and large groups.

1. The student is completely insecure about his paper.
2. The student blames you for his bad grades.
3. The student is anxious and tries to hide it by continually joking.
4. The student does not think she needs to come to the writing center.
5. The student does not think you are competent.
6. The student has not spent enough time preparing his paper.
7. The teacher's comments on the student paper are extremely unsupportive.
8. The assignment is difficult to figure out.

Other situations suitable for role playing or at least worth thinking about are
tutoring sessions in which you might feel uncomfortable such as when a student
is persistently silent, unwilling to respond, no matter what you say or do. You
ask a question, and the student does not answer. Uneasy with the heavy silence,
you rush in to answer the question yourself. The student merely nods, or worse,
sits there stonefaced. Once again, there is silence. You try again. No response.
Despite your best efforts, you feel completely ineffectual.

In a situation such as this, when the student does not respond immediately
to a comment or a question, Arkin and Shollar recommend counting to ten before
rushing in to answer the question yourself. "Give students enough time to gather
their thoughts so they can answer your questions (or their own) or comment on
the subject matter" (97), they advise. They also recommend allowing time after a
student answers a question so that he or she can reflect further before you ask
another one. "Rushing in to fill empty space, which new tutors do at times out of
anxiety or frustration, will only close down the lines of communication and make
tutoring a one way process" (Arkin and Shollar 97). Of course, if the student
never responds, you might want to try something else (other than shaking the
student by the shoulders) such as assigning a specific writing task. The main
point, though, is that you, yourself, should not feel as if you are a failure if the
student chooses not to respond. This happens to everyone.

Another situation to anticipate is that in which you, yourself, do not know
the answer to a student's question. The student asks and suddenly your mind
becomes blank or confused. If you are new to tutoring, this can be a terrifying

experience. However, it is important to keep in mind that not even the most distinguished professors can be expected to know everything. It is perfectly acceptable to show a student that sometimes tutors have to look something up or occasionally ask for help. Say something like, "I'm not too sure about that, and I don't want to mislead you. But let's ask one of the other tutors."

*Exercise*

With a partner, role play a situation in which the student doesn't respond immediately to the tutor's questions or in which the tutor doesn't know the answer to a question. How does it feel? Will you be able to handle these situations without panicking?

# Prepare for Tutoring by Practicing Non-Directive Listening

Carl Rogers, discussing important skills for counselors to develop, states that one of the most important is the ability to listen *with* the speaker, hearing what is said from his or her point of view and thus come to an understanding of what the speaker means. Rogers terms this type of listening "non-directive listening," which can only be conveyed through feedback in which you communicate or reflect exactly what you have heard, so that both you and the student know that what you heard is what he or she meant. A good way to practice non-directive listening is to practice paraphrasing what you hear—putting the student's comments or questions in other words, so that they know that they are being heard. Here is an example:

**Student:** I just can't relate to this topic.
**Tutor:** You don't know very much about the topic. This must worry you.

*Exercise*

Paraphrase the following comments, reading both sets of comments aloud.

**Student:** It doesn't matter what I do. I won't get a good grade.
**Tutor:**
**Student:** I don't care anything at all about nuclear power. What a boring topic!
**Tutor:**

## Listening for the Feeling

Rogers points out that when you listen with empathy, you do not merely repeat the words of the speaker. You must also indicate that you are aware of the feeling behind the statement. For example, if the student says, "I got another 'C' on the paper. I just can't write," you might say, "You must be feeling discouraged."

*Exercise*

Write or role play a response to the following student comments:

**Student:** The teacher hates me.
**Tutor:**

**Student:** The topic was too boring for me to work on.
**Tutor:**

**Student:** I'll never have to write much anyway. Why worry about it.
**Tutor:**

# Anticipating Tutoring by Analyzing the Effect Your Responses Are Likely to Have on Students

Sometimes, through chance or intuition, your responses to students are just right. You somehow "sense" the most appropriate thing to say. But sometimes, how you respond to a student can unintentionally generate negative feelings, cutting off, rather than facilitating communication. To prepare for tutoring, then, you can postulate a number of ways tutors can respond to students and imagine what effect they are likely to have.

For example, consider the following situation:

You are sitting in the writing center waiting for your next student, when Scott, a student with whom you have worked twice before, comes storming in. He throws his books upon a nearby table and walks over to you holding a crumpled paper.

"You look as if something is wrong," you observe.

"You're right about that," Scott snaps. "I came to the writing center *two times* last week and I *still* got a "C" on my paper. Coming here has been a total waste of time!"

You can respond to Scott in a number of ways, but the type of response you choose will be likely to generate a corresponding response in Scott. Let us look at some of these responses and the effect they are likely to have.

1. You can respond to Scott with **denial.**

   *"Oh come on, Scott. A grade isn't everything."*

   **Effect** By denying Scott's feelings, you might make him feel belittled, put down. Even when you say it nicely or in a friendly way, your message is clear: what is important to Scott is not that important in reality and not worth getting so upset about. This sort of response does not encourage Scott to continue talking to you. He is likely to walk out, maybe even more angry than he was.

2. You can respond to Scott by **questioning.**

   *"Why is it so important to you to get good grades?"*

   **Effect** This response puts Scott in the position of having to define his feelings, and he may feel put down or misunderstood. He is likely to argue to justify his position.

3. You can respond to Scott by **sharing your own experience:**

   *"That reminds me of something that once happened to me when I was in college. I worked for days on a paper and still got a "C." Just hang in there. You'll do better on the next paper. Just keep up the good work!"*

   **Effect** This response could be encouraging to Scott but still denies the feelings that the speaker is expressing. It offers "surface optimism," which Scott may or may not believe.

4. You can respond to Scott by **giving advice:**

   *What you need to do is get an early start on the next paper. Then maybe you'll be able to write a better paper."*

   **Effect** This response insinuates that Scott's paper wasn't really that good (maybe it wasn't!) or that Scott didn't work hard enough and may well have deserved the "C." If Scott feels that he has already worked as hard as he can on his paper, he may feel that no matter what he does, he'll never get a good grade.

5. You can respond to Scott by **criticizing or moralizing:**

   *"Well, if you had worked up a decent draft before you came here, we could have made more progress."*

   **Effect** This response might make you feel better, but it is likely to make Scott feel angry. He will not feel as though his feelings have been understood or accepted and he will probably argue defensively.

6. You can respond to Scott by **changing the subject:**

   "What's the topic for your next paper?"

   **Effect** With this response, once again, Scott may feel as if he has not really been heard or understood. The focus is taken away from his feelings and their sources.

7. You can make an **"I feel" statement.**

   *"I'm really sorry you didn't get the grade you wanted."*

   **Effect** This response conveys caring, but takes the focus off Scott and does not encourage him to continue. More importantly, it does not encourage him to use his setback productively and assume greater responsibility for his next paper.

8. You can clarify Scott's feelings by **reflecting what he is saying.**

   *"You worked hard on that paper and you're angry that it received a low grade. You must be disappointed."*

   **Effect** This response allows Scott to feel that he has been heard and understood. Your recognition of his feelings might encourage discussion, rather than self-justification. Scott might even decide to work harder on the next paper.

Obviously, I am arguing in behalf of response #8, in which you reflect Scott's feelings, encourage him to explore the situation, and then, hopefully, decide to work even harder on his next assignment. Of course, there is no guarantee that any response will motivate the desired behavior, though. All you can do is to be aware of which responses are likely to work.

In summary, then, you can anticipate writing by:

1. Being a writer yourself,
2. Reflecting on your own writing process,
3. Reflecting on collaboration and evaluation,
4. Becoming aware of how you respond to others,
5. Anticipating as many situations as possibly that might come up when you tutor.

Anticipating tutoring in these ways will help you approach your first real tutorial session with insight and confidence.

# Works Cited

Arkin, Marian and Barbara Shollar. *The Tutor Book.* New York: Longman, 1982.

Bruffee, Kenneth. "Collaborative Learning and the Conversation of Mankind." *College English* 46 (1984): 635–652.

Clark, Irene Lurkis. "Collaboration and Ethics in Writing Center Pedagogy." *Writing Center Journal* IX, 1 (Fall/Winter 1988): 3–13.

___"Maintaining Chaos in the Writing Center: A Critical Perspective on Writing Center Dogma." *Writing Center Journal* XI, 1 (Fall/Winter 1990): 81–95.

Hodges, Karen. "The Writing of Dissertations: Collaboration and Ethics." Paper Given at the Conference on College Composition and Communication. Atlanta, March 1987.

Trimbur, John. "Peer Tutoring: A Contradiction in Terms." *The Writing Center Journal* 7.2 (1987): 21–28.

# Chapter Three

# Working With Students:
# The Nature of the Writing Center Conference

A writing center conference is a bit like an egg—a lot is packed into it and one hopes that something useful and possibly even attractive will emerge (perhaps a well-formed chicken, maybe a gourmet omelette). Of course, there is no one model for a "successful" conference, and even if there were, it would be difficult, if not impossible, to replicate on a regular basis, since the quality of each conference is determined to a great extent by the interaction between the particular student and tutor. However, a few ideas concerning student-tutor interactions do pertain to most writing center conferences. These are the following:

1. Students and tutors should work together. The tutor does not monopolize the conference while the student just sits there nodding.

2. Students should come away from the conference having gained an understanding of at least one strategy for improving their texts (or if they have not brought a text, they understand the requirements of the assignment and/or have generated some ideas).

3. Students should come away from the conference having gained some insight into their strengths and weaknesses as writers. They have acquired a better understanding of what facets of the writing process they should work on and a concept of how to approach a subsequent writing task more effectively.

4. Students should come away from the conference feeling comfortable about using the writing center. They are likely to come again.

Admittedly, to reach all of these goals all of the time amid the often hurried (and harried) atmosphere in the writing center is not always possible. Nevertheless, as you begin to work with students in the writing center, you might keep them in mind.

## What Is Helpful for Students?

Although there has been much speculation about what factors contribute most significantly to improvement in student writing ability, two that are generally acknowledged are *motivation* and *practice* (not a big surprise). Common sense suggests that a student who really wants to learn how to write and who feels comfortable about trying out ideas and learning from mistakes is more likely to improve than one who is hostile to the whole notion of writing or who worries so much about making a mistake that he or she is unable to write at all. It is, therefore, extremely important for teachers or tutors in the writing center to develop a comfortable working relationship with their students, one that encourages students to experiment with their writing and to return to the writing center with multiple drafts.

Suppose, then, that this is your first day of tutoring in the writing center. You approach your first conference with enthusiasm, but also with a bit of anxiety. Although you have read a great deal about composition theory and are a good writer yourself, you wonder what you can do to develop a comfortable and productive working relationship with students. The suggestions in this chapter are designed to help you.

## Put the Student at Ease

When students first come to the writing center, it is important to put them at ease. Fearing ridicule or unfavorable evaluation, many students are terribly embarrassed to show their writing to anyone, particularly someone who seems to be in a position of authority. Some of them may feel that the very fact that they have even come to the writing center indicates that they are "remedial" or poorly qualified in some way. Some of them may have had unpleasant experiences with former teachers. Thus, the first encounter they have with a writing center tutor can do a great deal either to dispel or to reinforce such anxieties. As Rogers has discovered in clinical therapy, "the more a student feels that the environment is safe for personal thinking and feeling, the less tentative become the contributions, the more accelerated the momentum, the profounder the insights and self-satisfaction" (cited in Mandel 626).

CHOOSE AN APPROPRIATE SEATING ARRANGEMENT

So when that first student approaches you with a crumpled paper and a referral form, remember that she is probably a lot more nervous than you are. Introduce yourself, ask the student some friendly questions about classes, the assignment, why she has come, what needs to be done, what difficulties she has experienced thus far. Above all, indicate by your body language (smiling, offering your hand, looking comfortable and relaxed), as well as by your words, that you are there to *help* the student, not to judge her, that you approve of working through a paper in multiple drafts and that you recognize that writing is a difficult task, no matter how good a writer one might be. Help the student understand that most writers are not "inspired" and that it is not unusual for even professional writers to work hard to generate acceptable writing.

In the following interchange, for example, Tutor Jim indicates to Student Jane that he understands that students are sometimes under a great deal of pressure and do not allow enough time for planning a draft.

**Jim (tutor):** Did you have a plan or outline for this paper before you wrote it?
**Jane (Student):** No, I just wrote it. I didn't have much time to work on it.
**Jim:** (smiles and nods): A "night before" job, eh? Sometimes that happens to all of us.

This interchange can be contrasted with the following:

**Tim (tutor):** Did you have a plan or outline for this paper before you wrote it?
**Jane (Student):** No, I just wrote it. I didn't have much time to work on it.

**Tim:** You should always write an outline before you begin to write. Otherwise your work is going to be disorganized.

This second interchange is not only unnecessarily authoritarian and moralistic, it is also unlikely to produce any change in the student (after all, what can the student do about her lack of outline at this point?) Moreover, it erroneously suggests that outlining is an essential stage in the writing of all students, a notion that many would question.

## Get a Sense of the Student's Writing Process

To work effectively with students in the writing center, you should try to help students develop an effective writing process, not simply to improve a given text. It is therefore a good idea to find out how long the student has been working on the paper, what difficulties he or she may have experienced in writing it, and whether or not these are difficulties that the student has experienced before. Knowing how much time and effort have been put into a draft will help determine what sort of assistance the student might need, since a problematic draft may reflect lack of effort, lack of skill or both. A writer who brings in a disorganized, unfocused draft that was dashed off minutes before the conference may be quite different from a writer that has labored for a week over an equally disorganized, unfocused draft. The drafts may be similar in quality, but the writers are likely to have different abilities, requiring different approaches. To work effectively with students in the writing center, you should try to determine what sort of effort their papers represent.

You can find out how the student wrote the draft simply by asking friendly questions such as "When did you start this paper?" or "Tell me how you went about writing it?" You can also ask the student what he or she wants to work on, what difficulties were encountered, and what attempts were made to solve them. Or you can use a "Writing Process Report" that the student can fill out either before the conference or even while you are looking over a draft (it will give the student something to do instead of simply sitting there watching you read). In asking the student to fill out the form, though, make sure that you emphasize that you are using it simply to gain a greater understanding of what the student might need. Assure the student that you will not use it to assign a grade or make a judgment. A copy of the form follows.

# WRITING PROCESS REPORT

*Writing Center conferences are more effective when you and the tutor not only analyze and improve a text but also work to improve your writing process.*

*Therefore, while you are waiting, please take a few minutes to respond to the following questions:*

1. How much time did you spend in prewriting for this essay? How much time in <u>writing and revising</u> it?

   Hours prewriting:_____

   Hours Writing/Revising_____

2. Describe your <u>prewriting activities</u>. What did you do to invent ideas for the paper, select the ones you wanted to use, and plan some tentative structure for your essay?

3. Describe your <u>revision activities</u>. What global (i.e., largescale changes did you make in your plan or in your drafts? How carefully did you check your style and syntax?

4. What <u>problems</u> did you encounter in writing this paper? How did you attempt to solve them?

5. What would you like to focus on during this conference?

# Find Out When the Paper Is Due

The kind of work you decide to do with students in a writing center conference is determined, to some extent, by when the paper is due. If the student comes in well before a paper deadline, you will have a lot of time to develop ideas, generate drafts, and revise. Unfortunately, however, students don't always come to the writing center well in advance. In fact, some of them come in and tell you that the paper is due in an hour! How do you respond when the student tells you this? Here are two interchanges to examine:

**Tutor:** When is the paper due?
**James:** Um. In about two hours. Right after lunch.
**Tutor:** Well, I don't know why you bothered coming in. What do you expect I can do for you when the paper is due in two hours?

In this interchange, the tutor has make it clear that James should have brought his paper in earlier, and of course, the tutor is right. However, the problem with saying so in this manner is that James is likely to become defensive; in fact, he may walk out. So either the conference is going to begin on a note of hostility or else there may be no conference at all. Feeling rebuked by the tutor, James may never return to the writing center (unless he is required to come, in which case, he will come reluctantly); thus, he will miss out on valuable writing center instruction

To avoid generating a defensive reaction, you might respond to James like this:

**Tutor:** When is the paper due?
**James:** Um. In about two hours. Right after lunch.
**Tutor:** Well, it would have been better if you had come in with the paper earlier. We could have really worked on it then. But I'll be happy to look at it with you and see what sort of things you might work on for the next paper.

In this second interchange, the tutor did not make James feel foolish or angry, so perhaps he might bring his paper in earlier the next time. Another way the tutor could have responded is to ask James if he has the paper on a disk and has easy access to a computer. If James says "yes," James might say, "Well, let's look at the paper together and see what sort of revisions we might be able to make in a short time" (if there are computers in the writing center, they might revise directly on the screen). Even if they can only revise part of the paper, any resulting improvements might encourage James to come in more promptly with his next paper. The other possibility is for the tutor to ask James if he might be able to get an extension on the paper. If James says "yes," then he and the tutor will be able to begin to work seriously.

## Help Students Assume Responsibility for Their Own Work

For students and tutors to work together productively, it is important that students assume responsibility for their own work right from the beginning. If one views writing as a decision making process, then the goal of writing instruction must be to enable students to judge the appropriateness of the decisions they make as writers, insights that they will be able to apply to subsequent writing tasks. The teaching of a skill such as writing, like the teaching of any skill such as drawing or piano playing, is quite different from presenting a content area such as history or literature, and few would disagree that the goal of writing instruction involves a great deal more than merely teaching students to write in a specific way at a specific time.

However, students often view the writing center simply as a place where they can obtain "help" with a particular paper, and too often, the tutor allows the "quick fix" approach to determine the focus of the conference. Because "traditional educational practices emphasize student passivity and assume that the teacher is the omniscient giver of truth and knowledge" (Hunkins XII), new tutors will often conduct conferences by *telling* students how to revise their papers, rather than guiding them to discover how to do it for themselves. Of course, it is quicker and easier to tell students, rather than to guide them, but tutor dominated conferences, instead of producing autonomous student writers, usually produce students who remain totally dependent upon the teacher or tutor, unlikely ever to assume responsibility for their own writing. This sort of relationship is counterproductive to the goal of writing instruction.

In establishing a working relationship with students, it is therefore advisable for the teacher or tutor to begin their conferences by asking students which areas they, themselves, wish to emphasize, rather than merely reading their papers and suggesting revisions. For instance, the following two excerpts illustrate two approaches to conferencing, only one of which is geared toward helping students take responsibility for their own work.

*Excerpt #1*

**Sarah:** This is an essay my teacher told me to revise. I'm, not sure what's wrong with it.

**Phillip:** What do you think is wrong with it? Can you suggest a few areas to work on?

*Excerpt #2*

**Beth:** I really want to get a good grade in Comp. but I don't know what I'm doing wrong.

**Stan:** (takes about two minutes to read the paper silently) Hmnn, yes, I can see a few problems that are really interfering with your writing. You have a good vocabulary, that's obvious, but there are some basic problems of structure and style. It'll take some work, though. In other words, we can clear up your problems if you're willing to spend a fair amount of time in the lab.

In the first excerpt, one may note that Phillip did not immediately assume responsibility for the revision and that he indicated right away that the student would have to think about this matter for herself. But in the second interchange, Stan assumed immediate control, instantly diagnosing problems and recommending solutions. Moreover, the solutions offered were depicted as time consuming and tedious, more likely to discourage Beth than to motivate her to revise her work.

Putting students at ease and helping them assume responsibility for their own work can also be facilitated through the seating arrangement you choose for your conferencing session. It is generally known that certain positions tend to acquire symbolic value and to be associated with fixed roles, particularly those that place the tutor in a position of authority, the student in one of submission. Since these roles are sometimes associated with previous unsuccessful encounters with teachers, these roles can be counterproductive to the ultimate goal of tutoring—that is, to have students assume final responsibility for their own writing progress.

To counteract the undesirable effects of fixed role positions, it is best for students and teachers to sit side by side at a table, each holding a pencil. Sitting across from one another reinforces distance, rather than camaraderie, and is also impractical for working together, in that one always has to be reading upside down.

# Begin the Conference So As to Maximize Student Involvement

After you put the student at ease and ask some friendly questions to determine what sort of writer the student might be and what sort of effort was involved, you will want to begin discussion on some aspect of the text (or if there is no text, to generate ideas on the topic), that is, to begin the conference. How you begin conferences and the method you use to gain entrance into the text can have an impact on student involvement, so in addition to asking the student what he or she wishes to work on, here are a few suggestions to maximize student involvement:

1. Ask the student to explain the assignment to you. Then ask them to explain how they attempted to fulfill the assignment. This approach is likely to lead to a discussion of thesis and means of support.

2. If you decide to read the text silently (and some tutors prefer to do this in order to gain a greater understanding of its strengths and weaknesses), have the student write responses to the following questions:

   • The main point (or thesis) of my paper is_____.
   • I have supported this point with the following subpoints or examples:
   _____.

   Having the student write responses to these questions (or to other questions) while you read the paper will

   • give the student something to do, aside from simply sitting there looking uncomfortable,
   • direct the student's attention toward the focus and structure of the text,
   • provide a point at which discussion can begin, and
   • communicate the impression immediately that the student must get involved in the conference.

   While you are reading silently, you can also ask students to fill out the "Writing Process Report" discussed above.

3. You or the student can read all or part of the paper aloud (some students feel awkward reading aloud, in which case, you can read to the student as he or she comments on the text). Reading aloud can also provide a point of entrance, since problematic sections will become apparent. One helpful strategy is to ask the student to read the introduction aloud and point to the main point or thesis. Another is to have the student point to the section of the text he or she likes best or least.

# Be Aware of How Much You Are Talking

Another way to maximize student involvement in the conference is to think about the amount of talking it is desirable for the tutor and the student to do. In any tutoring or teaching situation, there is a tendency for the tutor or teacher to monopolize the conversation; after all, it is the teacher or tutor who has the information to impart and it is he or she who is directing the session. Moreover, often students have difficulty articulating ideas and are unaccustomed to discoursing at length about their work. However, as anyone who has had teaching or tutoring experience knows, when the tutor or teacher gives a mini-lecture during a conference there is a tendency for students to withdraw their attention. Often they fidget in their seats or glance nervously around the room. More significantly, they stop listening to what the tutor is saying and take little responsibility for the success of the conference. Therefore, in order to maximize student attention and responsibility, it is important to generate a substantial amount of student participation.

This issue is worth considering. Assuming one had total control over the conference, how much student participation would be desirable? Presumably, it would not be advantageous for the student to talk all of the time. Similarly, what percentage of the conference should be devoted to "teacher talk?" Obviously, the tutor has to do at least some of the talking.

My own feeling on this is that tutors should talk *somewhat* more than students, but not so much as to monopolize the session. The main idea to keep in mind is that learning is most likely to occur when students discover ideas for themselves. If possible, don't simply tell students what to do or simply do it for them, no matter how satisfying or efficient it might be for you to do so.

For example, Jason came to the writing center with the paper you analyzed at the end of chapter one. Reread the assignment and the paper. Then note the lack of thesis development in the paper and how it does not really fulfill the requirements of the assignment. Now observe how tutor, Cynthia, attempted to deal with these problems.

### Cynthia's Conference With Jason:

**Cynthia (tutor):** Okay, well, I've read your paper and I think you really need to look at the assignment again. From your introduction, I have the impression that you are going to talk about how the electronic media have harmed society.

**Jason:** Right. That was the assignment.

**Cynthia:** Yeah, but then you go on to talk about how unrealistic some of these shows are. And that's okay. But you don't say anything about why unrealistic shows are harmful. You haven't really fulfilled the requirements of the assignment.

**Jason:** Oh.

**Cynthia:** And then in the conclusion, you don't say anything about the harm caused to society. Most of your paper is simply a list of examples. It doesn't really talk about the assignment, does it?

Note that Cynthia took a highly active role in the conference, telling Jason what the difficulties were, rather than leading him to discover them for himself. The fact that the tutor monopolized the session can be easily seen from a glance at the format. The tutor sections were discursive; the student sections were brief.

Note also that Cynthia was unnecessarily authoritarian in her presentation, discoursing about the problems in the paper and asking a rhetorical question, almost as if she were chastising Jason for not following through on the thesis stated in the introduction. Jason is likely to feel quite intimidated by Cynthia's tone.

Now contrast Cynthia's conference with that of Bonnie:

### Bonnie's Conference With Jason:

**Bonnie:** Tell me about your paper. What is your main idea or thesis?

**Jason:** My paper is about how television can be harmful to society because of stereotypes.

**Bonnie:** Okay. Good. That's what the assignment required. Now can you read me the sentence in the first paragraph where you state that idea?

(Jason reads the last sentence in the first paragraph)

**Bonnie:** Okay, Good. That's clear. Now, would you please read me the second paragraph.

(Jason reads it aloud)

**Bonnie:** Hmn. That paragraph has some good ideas in it. But I think I feel a little confused. What was your thesis again?

**Jason:** That t.v. has harmed society.

**Bonnie:** Right. The way I understand the main point of your essay, the key word here is "harmed." But the paragraph you just read—do you see what is confusing me?

**Jason:** Well, okay. I think you might be confused because I talk about all these shows. Maybe you aren't familiar with them.

**Bonnie:** Actually, I do know some of them, and, anyway, I think you give me a pretty good idea of what they are about. But . . . let's look closely at that paragraph. What's you main point there?

**Jason:** Oh, I see. I think I'm showing how unrealistic those shows are. But I don't use the word 'harm' in that paragraph.

**Bonnie:** Good. Can you see why I was confused.

**Jason:** Yeah. I talk about stereotypes, but not about harm to society.

**Bonnie:** Right. That's the link I was looking for. Now read the next paragraph. Oh, and glance at the conclusion as well.

**Jason:** I don't believe it. I don't talk about harm in that paragraph or the conclusion either. I'm really wandering away from the topic. So now what do I do? Do I have to start all over again?

**Bonnie:** No. I don't think so. You've got some very good examples here. But you have to link those examples to your main point or thesis. So let's do a cluster to get some more connection. You talk about unrealistic stereotypes. Let's get some ideas down about why these might be harmful.

One might note the following about the second interchange:

1. Unlike Cynthia, Bonnie assumed the role of audience. Because she asked clarifying questions, Jason had to explain what he was attempting to achieve in his paper.

2. Bonnie was supportive of Jason. She praised him for his examples and his understanding of the requirements of the assignment.

3. Bonnie did not monopolize the conference. She and Jason took turns talking. She also insured that Jason became an active participant in the conference by having him read aloud and by asking questions requiring a thoughtful answer (Can you see why I was confused?).

4. Bonnie *led* Jason to understand the lack of connection in his paper. She did not merely lecture to him about it.

5. Bonnie suggested a specific, manageable strategy to help develop connection between the thesis and the examples. Jason is much more likely to undertake revision if he has a sense of how to begin.

## Ask Questions—Don't Provide Answers

Another way you can involve the student actively in the writing center conference is to ask questions designed to stimulate thinking. Questioning can provide students with an opportunity to explore topics and argue points out view. Effective questioning can also give the writing center tutor immediate information about student comprehension and learning. Jacobs and Karliner point out that "the way the student and tutor perceive their roles in a writing conference— either as students and teacher or as two conversants—in large part determines whether the conference results in significant change in the cognitive level of the revision or merely in a patching of the rough draft" (489).

In order for the writing conference to be used to maximum effectiveness, then, writing center teachers and tutors must learn to discard their traditional roles as information givers and allow students to become equal participants. This shift in emphasis necessitates their learning to ask "open" questions, those designed to generate a wide range of response, maximizing student involvement, as opposed to "closed" questions, those requiring only one word answers, "yes," "no," or "oh." Try to phrase your questions so as to motivate students to think for themselves and to view the choices they make as their own. They will, then, hopefully, attribute the success of their revision not to the skill of the tutor, but to their own emerging abilities.

Actually, one of my favorite questions is "so what?" or "why does that matter?" These questions help students think about the audience or readers of their papers and of the importance of choosing issues that will move readers to change their minds about a topic or at least think about the topic in a new way. Since no one wants to read a paper that tells them nothing new, the question "so what" can stimulate thinking about the implications of a thesis. Here is an example:

**Mark (tutor):** Okay, you claim that a lot of t.v. shows are unrealistic. You say that t.v. promotes racial stereotypes and show all the women as being beautiful. But so what? So what if t.v. is unrealistic?

**Jason:** Well, it makes people think about other races as nasty. And we all have to live together, you know. If I think about someone from another race as being a criminal, I'm not going to want to be around that person.

In this interchange, Mark's question, "so what?," stimulated Jason to think about the connection between stereotypes and societal harm. Considering the implications of his point is likely to lead him to work on developing the missing connection in his paper.

Questioning strategies can also be used to reduce ego threat, an aspect of conferencing of particular relevance to anxious writers. In conferring with such students, it is particularly important for tutors to make the atmosphere as comfortable as possible, and one way to do this is to present unfamiliar material in the guise of the familiar. Thus, instead of pointing out the comma splices in the paper of the basic writer, or asking the student if he or she knows what a comma splice is, it is more effective to phrase questions within a familiar context and include necessary definitions in a prefatory statement. For example, one might alert a student to the comma splices in his paper as follows:

A lot of students have a habit of putting two sentences together by means of a comma, which is incorrect, instead of by a period or a word such as "and" or "but." Can you find examples of such comma splices in your paper?

This sort of question reduces anxiety by providing a definition that the student must know in order to correct the paper, without calling attention to the fact that the student might not be familiar with it.

Establishing a good working relationship between tutors and students has long been a given of all tutorial instruction; however, defining what constitutes such a relationship and specifying behaviors and approaches that best insure that such a relationship will develop have usually been left to intuition. Thinking in advance about the goals of the conference and about how to realize these goals will make it more likely that your conferences will be successful.

# Works Cited

Hunkins, Francis. *Involving Students in Questioning.* Allyn and Bacon, Inc.: Boston, 1976.

Jacobs, Suzanne and Adlea B. Karliner. "Helping Student Writers to Think: The Effects of Speech Roles in Individual Conferences on the Quality of Thought in Student Writing." *College English* 38 (January 1977): 489–506.

Mandel, Barrett John. "Teaching Without Judging." *College English* 34 (February 1973): 623–634.

# Chapter Four

# Working With Students: Interpreting Assignments, Developing Ideas

*"I don't know what the teacher wants."*
*"I'm totally confused by this assignment."*
*"I can't think of anything to write about."*

When you work in a writing center, you will often hear students make statements such as these. In fact, one of the most common reasons students come to the writing center is that they are confused by their writing assignments and/or can't come up with workable ideas for their papers. Sometimes, students will recount horror stories of nail chewing, paper-wadding all night vigils, resulting in frustration, rather than in inspiration. They may tell you that their confusion and anxiety has caused them to develop writing block, so that they are unable to write anything at all. Or they may manage to write a draft or part of a draft but then discover that it doesn't fulfill the requirements of the assignment or that it says very little, because they have little understanding of the writing task. Helping students understand assignments and generate ideas for papers is one of the most important functions a writing center can fulfill.

Working with students on interpreting assignments and generating ideas can be extremely rewarding, but it requires patience and understanding. Confronted with student after anxious student, puzzled, blank of mind, and abandoned of hope, frustrated tutors are often tempted to throw up their hands and exclaim, "They just don't know how to think!" or "They have no imagination!" or, worse, "They're not intelligent enough to think through an assignment." I urge you, though, not to yield to this temptation. Instead, try to figure out the source of the problem. Then work with them on interpreting assignments and developing prewriting strategies.

## Interpreting Assignments

Probably the most common reason that students are confused by a writing assignment is that they don't read it carefully and spend too little time thinking about it. They simply glance at it, perhaps get a sense of the topic to be addressed, and then wait until the last minute to begin writing, without examining it further. One basic point to stress in working with students on assignments, is the importance of reading the assignment slowly and beginning to think about it well in advance of when it is due.

However, even when students read their assignments carefully, they sometimes become confused because they are unfamiliar with the terminology used and/or with the characteristics of the type of paper they are expected to write. It is therefore not surprising that they are unable to write or that they generate papers that talk *around* a topic instead of addressing the assignment directly. Of course, sometimes, the assignments themselves are the source of the problem, many of them so ambiguously and confusingly written that it is unlikely that *anyone* would understand them (at a recent conference, such assignments were referred to as "assignments from hell").

Most assignments can be figured out, however, and I suggest that when an assignment is causing confusion that you begin to help the student understand it by completing the following steps:

1. The student should read the assignment aloud.
2. The student should point to key terms in the assignment that tell what it is that he or she must do in order to write the paper.
3. Work with the student to isolate the task that the assignment requires.
4. Discuss implicit requirements that may not be directly stated, but which are necessary in order for the assignment to be completed satisfactorily.

Working through these steps will help the student understand the requirements of the assignment. Then you can then work on prewriting strategies to develop ideas.

*Applying Theory to Practice*

As an example of this process, let us examine the following assignment that Alison brought in to the writing center:

_____ **Writing Topic** _____

*Writers of advertisements, whether for television, radio, magazines, or newspapers, have had a profound impact on our society, often shaping the way in which we think and influencing our standards and values. In particular, advertising has had an especially strong influence on our concept of male and female attractiveness, and, as a result, our ideal image of beauty and/or masculinity has become equated with the men and women depicted in ads.*

*Think about this influence, and choose an advertisement from a magazine. Study the ad carefully, making note of as many details as possible. Then write a three page essay in which you address the following question:*

> *How does your ad reflect (or refute) an ideal image of beauty and/or masculinity? How is this image being used to sell the product?*

Alison came to the writing center because she was confused by the assignment and had written a preliminary draft with which she was not satisfied. "I'm not sure this paper is what the teacher wants," said Alison. "I started writing this draft, but then I got all mixed up and couldn't finish it. Its really disorganized and doesn't say very much." Here is the draft that Alison wrote:

Since magazines were first published, they have become an important part of our culture. They provide us with many different types of information, such as news, and introduce us to new ideas. Magazines help communicate these ideas, not only through their articles but also because of advertisements.

There are many magazines in our society and there are many advertisements, especially advertisements for women such as perfume, clothes, and cosmetics. Magazines also advertise merchandise that women like to buy. One ad that does this is the ad for "Blue Grass" perfume.

When we turn to this ad, we are at first confused. We see a beautiful woman with a slender figure. She is completely naked without even one stitch of clothing on. This is strange because the ad is for perfume. It seems as if there is no connection between the advertiser's product and a naked model. Of course, many advertisements use the same technique, especially motorcycle advertisements that sometimes show picture of new motorcycles surrounded by models wearing bathing suits.

Alison became stuck at this point because she could not see where her paper was going. "I'm supposed to say something about 'ideal beauty,' " she observed, "but I seem to be going off the track."

## Alison's Confusion

Like many students, Alison is confused about several requirements of the assignment, requirements that pertain to many college writing tasks. These are the following:

1. Alison did not understand that her assignment required her to develop a *thesis* or a main point. Generally, this is a requirement for most college writing assignments, although some of them do not state it directly.

2. Alison did not understand that her assignment contained the implicit directive to *establish a definition;* that is, before she could decide how the ad she had chosen either reflected or refuted a concept of ideal beauty, she had to define what that concept was. Most college writing assignments require definition of at least some terms, even if they do not specifically direct students to do so.

3. Alison did not understand that her assignment required her to analyze a *relationship,* that is, the relationship between what was in the ad and the concept of ideal beauty she had defined and the relationship between what was in the ad and the product the ad was trying to sell.

In addition to being confused about the requirements of her assignment, Alison had not used prewriting strategies to generate sufficient materials to develop her ideas. She had not examined her ad in sufficient detail, and so quickly became "stuck." Because she had little idea of what she wanted to say, she began by writing generalities that had little to do with her topic. The "throat clearing" in the first two paragraphs reflect Alison's lack of focus and purpose.

Alison's difficulties with this assignment, then, may be traced to her unfamiliarity with its requirements, many of which were not specifically stated in the assignment itself. One way that the writing center can be helpful to students such as Alison is to show them how to understand the language of assignments, so that they will know what sort of paper to write. Once they understand the assignment, you can then work with them on strategies for generating ideas.

## A Procedure for Working with Assignments

The following procedure can help students understand their writing assignments when they come to the writing center:

**1) It is helpful for students to** *circle all of the words in the assignment that seem especially important.* In Alison's assignment, key words such as "ideal beauty," "reflect" or "refute" should be examined and defined. The question "How is this image being used to sell the product? should be highlighted so that the student can decide if she understands what it means. In some instances, it is helpful for the student to rephrase the question and to examine questions implied by the main question in order to gain a better understanding of what is needed to fulfill the assignment. In Alison's assignment, the main question could be rephrased as "how does the ad work?" or "what concept of beauty is being represented in the ad?" The assignment also implied several other questions such as "How does the ad use this concept of ideal beauty to sell its product?"

**2) Help students understand that, in most cases, they will be developing** *a thesis or main point* **in their papers.** Although when they first begin working on their assignment, students may not know what that main point might be, they should be aware that eventually they will have to develop one. Even descriptive or narrative papers usually focus around a main point. One way to help students think about the main point of their papers is to have them complete the following sentence:

The purpose of my paper is to show (or prove) that_____.

At first, they may not be able to fill in the blank, and, of course, they may change their ideas many times as they begin to write. Nevertheless, it is useful for them to remember the importance of having a thesis or a main point.

**3) Help students understand that most college writing assignments contain the implicit requirement of** *defining terms.* Often, that definition will serve as a framework for the presentation of major points.

**4) Help students understand that most college writing assignments concern** *a relationship between ideas.* Perhaps the relationship between cause and effect (or the implications and consequences of an action or policy), a comparison or contrast, or an analysis of the relationship of a whole into its parts. These relationships can serve as a "heuristic," that is, as a mechanism for enabling students to generate ideas.

## Other Characteristics of College Writing Assignments

Alison was confused about her assignment because she did not realize that it required her to develop a thesis, define terms, and develop a relationship between ideas. Other aspects of college writing assignments that may confuse students and that writing center tutors should be aware of are as follows:

1. A suitable thesis for college writing assignments should have an *impact upon an intended audience*—that is, it ought to change their audience's beliefs about the topic, at least somewhat, perhaps even move the audience toward or against an action or policy. To help students think about the impact of their thesis on an audience, you might have them fill in these two sentences.

Before they read my paper, my audience thinks_____about my topic.

After they read my paper, my audience will think_____about my topic.

2. College writing assignments often expect that the student will understand that a topic or issue is **complex** and reflect that understanding in the paper by considering several perspectives on an issue and anticipating possible objections from a reader. This requirement is especially important if the student is expected to develop a position on a controversial issue for which there is no easy solution. Here is an example of a topic for which the student must indicate awareness of complexity:

*If we grant that law enforcement officers must sometimes use force in policing actions, where and how should the line be drawn between acceptable and unacceptable levels of force?*

To write intelligently on this topic, students must demonstrate awareness that this in an extremely complex topic, that on one hand, crime has increased, particularly in large cities, yet, on the other, that excessive police power could result in civil rights abuses. Note that this assignment also requires that students define what they mean by "acceptable" and "unacceptable" as applied to the use of force by police.

3. College writing assignments often require students to consider questions of **degree**. Many of them use phrases such as "to what extent" or "indicate the extent to which" meaning that students must respond in terms of an evaluation or judgment. Here is an example of such an assignment:

*A myth may be defined as a cultural belief that is largely invisible—unacknowledged or unquestioned—to those who accept it. For example, the myth of feminine inferiority made it seem as if women's subordination was part of the natural order, a biologically established, rather than a cultural condition. Because myths and cultural beliefs can destroy the ways in which people perceive the world, they can exert a harmful effect upon how such people think and act.*

## Writing Task

*Select a contemporary cultural myth that you consider to have a harmful effect upon society. Then in a well-supported essay, address the following writing task:*

> *To what extent is this myth harmful to society?\**

For this assignment, students must indicate that a given cultural myth is harmful to society *to some extent* or *to some degree*. Note that for this assignment, too, the student will have to use definition in order to establish the meaning of the word "harmful" in this context.

## For Further Exploration

1. Suppose you are working with Alison who is confused about her assignment discussed above. Write a dialogue between Alison and yourself in which you help her understand that she must define her terms and develop a thesis.

2. Below is the writing topic presented at the end of chapter I. Analyze this topic in terms of its requirements. Does it require the student to develop a thesis, define terms, postulate a relationship, demonstrate awareness of the complexity of an issue, or address the topic in terms of degree? Try to write a response to this topic yourself. Then discuss the requirements of this topic with a group of other tutors.

## Writing Topic

*There is no question that the electronic media—T.V., radio, movies—have profoundly influenced society in the twentieth century. The media have been seen as factors in everything from the creation of designer jeans to the election of the American president. Because of their influence, the electronic media have generated a great deal of debate regarding their potential for both good and evil.*

*In a well-written essay, address the following questions:*

> **Has the Influence of the Electronic Media Been Harmful to Society? Why or Why Not?**

*\*adapted from U.S.C.'s Freshman Writing Orientation Notebook, 1991.*

*In your response, you should focus on specific ways the media have influenced society. You may wish to consider one or two of the following issues: myths and illusions created by the media, racial and sexual stereotypes, consumerism, social values, political values, the depiction of crime and violence. However, you are not limited to these choices and are encouraged to select your own.\**

## Thinking About Assignments: A Form

At the end of this chapter is a form called "Thinking About Your Assignment," that you might find useful in helping students interpret assignments. Select one of the assignments reproduced in this book and use this form to respond to it.

# Developing Ideas

Even when students understand the purpose of their assignments, they still may experience difficulty in generating ideas; for such students, the non-threatening environment of the writing center provides a comfortable setting for experimenting with possibilities. Some students find that simply coming to the writing center and talking or brainstorming about a topic is sufficient to get them started. For others, more formal strategies may be more effective. Understanding why students have difficulty in generating ideas and helping them learn some strategies to help them is an important part of working in a writing center.

## Why Can't Students Think of Ideas for Their Papers?

James Adams in *Conceptual Blockbusting* feels that most of us, but particularly anxiety-ridden students are prevented from exploring ideas freely because of emotional blocks that inhibit us from doing so. A few of these blocks that are relevant to the problem students have in generating ideas for papers are as follows:

1. *The fear of taking a risk.* Adams points out that since most of us have grown up rewarded when we produce the "right answer" and punished if we make a mistake, that we tend to avoid risk whenever possible. Yet exploring ideas for papers means risk-taking, to some extent. To come up with anything new means considering, at least for a short time, a notion that has not been sanctioned before, a notion that one may later reject as inappropriate in some way. Because students fear the rejection associated with risk taking, they are often unable to entertain new ideas and will reject even a glimmer of creative though which may prove to be unsuitable and subject them to ridicule.

2. *No appetite for chaos.* Since the fear of making a mistake is rooted in insecurity, most of us tend to avoid ambiguity whenever possible, opting for safety over uncertainty, a condition Adams refers to as "having no appetite for chaos." Thus, because they are uncomfortable with the "chaos" which characterizes the stage in the writing process that exists before one generates an idea or focuses a topic, many students reach for order before they have given the topic sufficient exploration. Thus, they find themselves "stuck" with dead end or uninteresting topics.

3. *Preference for judging, rather than generating ideas.* This emotional block, according to Adams, also has its root in our preference for safety rather than for risk, producing in students a tendency to judge an idea too early or indiscriminately. Adams states, "If you are a compulsive idea-judger, you should realize that this is a habit that may exclude ideas from your own mind before they have had time to bear fruit" (47).

4. *Inability to Incubate.* There is general agreement that the unconscious plays an important role in problem solving, and it is therefore important for students to give their ideas an opportunity to incubate, to wrestle with a problem over several days. Yet students often procrastinate working on their papers until the day before they are due. They then find themselves blocked before they can even get started.

5. *Lack of motivation.* Students are often asked to write about topics in which they have little interest; their motivation lies only in the grade they hope to receive. Yet, as Adams points out, it is unlikely that students can come up with an interesting idea for a paper, if they aren't motivated, at least somewhat, by the topic itself.

Mike Rose, in *Writer's Block: The Cognitive Dimension,* suggests several related reasons for writer's block:

1. The rules by which students guide their composing processes are rigid, inappropriately invoked, or incorrect.
2. Students' assumptions about composing are misleading (such as "really good writing is inspirational and requires little effort.")
3. Students edit too early in the composing process, thus polishing surface instead of thinking freely.
4. Students lack appropriate planning and discourse strategies or rely on inflexible or inappropriate strategies.
5. Students invoke conflicting rules, assumptions, plans, and strategies (for example: "avoid the passive voice," and "keep the 'I' out of reports").
6. Students evaluate their writing with inappropriate criteria or criteria that are in adequately understood.[2]

For these, and probably for many other reasons, students have a hard time generating topics for their papers and of developing those topics to conclusion. What can writing center tutors do to help students in this problematic area?

## Encourage an Atmosphere of Freedom and Experimentation

Since students may be too unsure of themselves to explore the impractical and irrational side of human behavior necessary for creativity, they should be encouraged to experiment with new ideas, entertain possibilities for papers, without fear of ridicule or negative evaluation. It is therefore very important that the environment in a writing center be "hang-loose," as informal as possible without sacrificing seriousness of purpose. Have lots of scrap paper around, lots of pens and pencils. Talk about how many ideas you, yourself, toss out before you settle on one to develop. Empathize about how hard *everyone* finds the generation of new ideas. Encourage using scissors and paste; possibly work in groups to stimulate discussion. Whatever encourages students to explore new ideas and feel comfortable about doing so should be part of the prewriting environment.

## Help Students Understand That Discovery of a Main Topic or Subtopic Can Occur at Any Stage of the Writing Process

Many students do not develop their topics adequately because they are under the impression that writing occurs in a series of linear stages: the student thinks about the topic, he prewrites, he writes, he revises, and he edits. However, it is now generally recognized that writing is a *recursive,* rather than a linear process. Although some students work in an orderly fashion from the generation of ideas to the production of sentences, others find new ideas while they are revising previous ones and often move back and forth between phases of the writing process. Flower and Hayes in *A Process Model of Composition* suggest that writing is characterized by "recursiveness" to allow for a "complex intermingling of stages" (46). Mike Rose adheres to the model proposed by Barbara and Fredrick Hayes Roth, which they have labeled "opportunism." They explain this model as follows.

> We assume that people's planning activity is largely *opportunistic.* That is, at each point in the process, the planner's current decisions and observations suggest various opportunities for plan development. The planner's subsequent decisions follow up on selected opportunities. Sometimes, these decision-sequences follow an orderly path and produce a neat top-down expansion. . . . However, some decisions and observations might also suggest less orderly opportunities for plan development (276).

As Mike Rose points out,

> applied to writing, opportunism suggests that the goals, plans, discourse frames, and information that emerge as a writer confronts a task are not always hierarchically sequenced from most general strategy to most specific activity. These goals, plans, frames, etc., can influence each other in a rich variety of ways; for example, while editing a paragraph, a writer may see that material can be organized in a different way or as a writer writes a certain phrase, it could cue other information stored in memory (9).

In the writing center, then, teachers and tutors can help students take advantage of these various opportunities which come along as they write. This means not being afraid to explore new ideas even in a half written draft or exploring directions not previously considered.

## Helping Students with Prewriting: Procedures and Strategies

Once students feel comfortable enough to experiment with new ideas and understand that the writing process is recursive, you can help them develop procedures and strategies to generate topics for papers. Below, are some ideas you might find useful in the writing center. Remember, though, that the key words concerning this area are *flexibility* and *variety*. No one strategy is best for all students and all assignments.

### Have Students Talk about Their Topics Before They Write

Robert Zoellner, in his article "Talk-Write: A Behavioral Pedagogy for Composition," states that students will write more clearly and expansively if they approach writing through other behavior (speaking) which has already proven at least reasonably successful. Zoellner bases this "principle of intermodal transfer" on two assumptions:

1. Students are better at talking than writing because they have had more practice.
2. They have the ability to improve their writing because, in trying to do so, they are already using a learned skill, talking.

Until fairly recently, Zoellner's ideas were only theoretical; several years ago, however, George Kennedy's work indicated that Zoellner's recommendations actually work, a validation for using prewriting conferences in the writing center. Kennedy divided a group of basic writers into two groups: the experimental "Speakwrites" and the control "Writeonlys," and both groups watched a film which was used as the stimulus for later exposition. The speakwrites were interviewed individually on the subject of the film and were then asked to write a 30 minutes

ENCOURAGE STUDENTS TO TALK
ABOUT THEIR TOPICS

essay on a general topic generated by the film, using the best techniques for writing they knew. The Writeonlys had no opportunity to discuss the film and were asked only to write the 30 minute essay, similarly being told to use the best techniques they knew. When the essays were graded by independent evaluators, the Speakwrites' essays received significantly higher scores than did the Writeonlys. In general, then, Kennedy's research suggests that writing center tutors can help students generate better ideas for papers by getting them to talk about their topics before they write.

### What Should Students Talk About?

Conferences in the writing center devoted to prewriting might focus on several issues related to the topic: student interest in the topic, motivation for writing about it, the perception of the reader, possible directions in which the paper can go, and, ultimately, the purpose of the paper, leading to the focusing of the thesis.

Suppose, for instance, that a student, Jennifer, has come into the writing center with the following assignment:

> *Pick a comic strip. Read back issues covering several weeks. Then write a three page typewritten essay in which you analyze the values represented by the major character or characters in this strip.*

All the student has with her is the comic section of the local newspaper and some very blank white paper. She has a vague idea that she wants to write about the comic strip, *Cathy*, but she hasn't focused her topic or developed a thesis. She also doesn't have a clear understanding of what the assignment entails. She says, "I don't know *what* I'm going to write about." Given this assignment, you might conduct an interchange along the following lines:

**Tutor:** I see you are thinking of using the comic strip "Cathy." Why did you choose that one?

**Jennifer:** Well, it's one of my favorites, and I can really relate to the character.

**Tutor:** I like it a lot too, But what do you mean, you can "relate" to it?

**Jennifer:** Well, Cathy is so much like a lot of people I know. I mean, girls in my classes and places like that. I guess she's a lot like me, too, when I come to think about it.

**Tutor:** In what way?

**Student:** Well, like she's always on a diet. But she makes a million excuses for breaking it. And then there's Irving, her boyfriend. She doesn't really know *what* to do with that relationship. She says she wants her freedom and a career. But then she, like, well, falls *apart* whenever he hints at love or gives her flowers or something.

**Tutor:** Sounds like you know a lot about the topic. Anything more you can tell me about Cathy?

**Student:** Well, she's always being taken advantage of. Her boss, yeah, he's always piling work on her, and she can't seem to say "no."

**Tutor:** Go on. Anything else?

**Student:** Yeah. Well, there's her parents, her mother, really. She really doesn't want to be like her mother, but she finds herself doing things her mother would do or worrying what her mother will say. I can really relate to that.

**Tutor:** All of these things sound very interesting to me. Do you think other people would be interested in a paper about "Cathy?"

**Jennifer:** Oh, yeah. Like all the girls in my sorority house like to read it. They can relate to it too.

**Tutor:** Good. So you have a subject and you know something about who would like to read about it, your audience or your readership. Now we have to focus your topic around the writing assignment. Let's reread what you have to do.
(Both reread the assignment)
Well, you have the character. Now let's see about the other word in the assignment that's important to think about.

**Jennifer:** You mean "analyze the values?" Yeah, I was wondering about that one.

**Tutor:** Do you know what is meant by values?

**Jennifer:** Not really.

**Tutor:** Well, next time it might be a good idea to ask your teacher about all points in the assignment before you begin to think about it. For now, though, let's assume that "values" means what a society considers right or wrong, good or bad.

**Jennifer:** Right. Okay. I think she said that in class. Like in Cathy's society, being thin and beautiful is so important that food and clothes have made everybody crazy.

**Tutor:** An obsession, you mean?

**Jennifer:** Right. And women don't know for sure what they are supposed to do with their lives. Like Cathy wants a career but she's worried that she won't be able to get married and have children like her mother did.

**Tutor:** Good points there. How about at work?

**Jennifer:** Well, Cathy wants to be a successful business woman. But she can't say "no" to men, because she's been brought up to be an obedient little girl. So she always has more work assigned than she wants to do. And she feels, well, like—*used*.

**Tutor:** It sounds as if you have a terrific women's issues paper here, using "Cathy" as an example of problems young women are facing and the way in which the values in our society affect women.

**Jennifer:** I'm not sure what you mean.

**Tutor:** Okay. Let's list all the issues you talked about on a sheet of paper. Then you can find examples in "Cathy" to illustrate what you are talking about.

**Jennifer:** Like talking about how important it is for a woman to be thin. And how women don't really know what they're supposed to be.

**Tutor:** Right. You have the idea. And once you've listed these examples and read a few more back issues, then see if you can answer these questions in writing: (Writes)

1. The purpose of my paper is to prove_____.
2. Before they read my paper, my audience thinks_____ about my topic.
3. After they read my paper, my audience will think_____ about my topic.

**Student:** Okay. I'll get back to you in a little while.

In this interchange, the tutor began by asking Jennifer to talk about what she knew about the topic, delineating issues that could be used in the paper. She then helped the student define the writing assignment, explored a possible direction for the paper, then gave her time to think about the purpose and focus she might want to develop. Hopefully, Jennifer will think some more about this topic so that she will be able to answer the questions with useful information.

The tutor in this interchange not only generated discussion on the topic; she also helped the student understand the writing assignment more clearly. This is a very useful approach for a prewriting conference, as very frequently students do not understand what is meant by some of the terms in the assignment and never get around to asking the classroom instructor for clarifications. As was discussed earlier in this chapter, terms such as "develop a thesis" or "analyze the values" are often misinterpreted by students, so they merely describe a topic in a general sense, recount the plot or scheme of a movie, television show, novel, or comic strip, without making any point at all. Even when the student has already written a draft, it is helpful to go back to the assignment and have the student underline all the key words—the words which are crucial to fulfilling the assignment. You can then find out if the student really understands the requirements or has explored the topic adequately. You can also help students discover whether or not they fully understand an assignment by having then fill in the form at the end of this chapter.

To reiterate the point of this section, then, a helpful way for writing center tutors to help students generate ideas for their papers is to engage then in purposeful conversation about the topic. Mack and Skjei, in *Overcoming Writing Blocks* similarly suggests that defining "in writing, as precisely as possible just what you're there to accomplish" will sharpen thinking and reduce anxiety, making the writing task "seem less intimidating" (79).

## Encourage Student to Do *Something* Before They Attempt to Write

Often students are unable to write because they have given no thought to the topic they are assigned. They hastily read the assignment, forget about it for a few days, and then, the night before it is due, sit down and chew their pencil. Yet few if any professional writers attempt to write in this way. Janet Emig, in 1964, collected data from both professional and academic writers, which revealed that although there was great diversity and individuality in planning practices, ranging from the elaborated outline to informal conversations with friends, all writers indicated that they engaged in "some form of planning prior to the production of planned discourse" (67). It makes sense, then, that students, too, could profit from learning a variety of flexible learning strategies, to which they can turn when faced with the ghastly white paper. The writing center tutor should instruct students on how to use some of these techniques and then allow students time to practice them.

### *What Kind of Prewriting Techniques Should a Writing Center Tutor Use?*

To generate thinking about what sort of prewriting techniques you should present to students in the writing center, consider how you, yourself, write papers for your classes. Do you jot down notes on scraps of paper? Do you do extensive research in the library? Do you use an outline? Do you work on a computer?

A number of useful prewriting strategies exist today and I will explain a few of them. But you as writing center tutor should decide which ones work best for you in dealing with students. No one technique is equally useful for everyone.

### Intuitive Versus Intellectual Approaches to Prewriting

Sabina Johnson divides prewriting strategies into the "intuitive" and the "intellectual." Intuitive approaches seek to generate ideas by "forcing the writer to dredge up from his unconscious the impressions stored there of the material" (235). Unstructured and seemingly haphazard, intuitive approaches require the writer to move from the material into the self, depending upon the interplay between the spontaneous utterances of the writer and the unconscious from which they emerge. Several "intuitive" approaches to prewriting include brainstorming, freewriting, and journal keeping.

Intellectual approaches, in contrast, depend on "a formal set of questions which the writer applies to her material much as she might hold up a prism to a beam of light so as to analyze it or break it down into components, from the study of which she may form an idea about the whole and its parts" (Johnson 235). Intellectual approaches require the writer to move from the self into the material. Intellectual approaches may also be referred to as *heuristics*, a heuristic being a technique for discovering ideas or finding solutions to problems. In my discussion of various heuristics, however, I will follow Ross Winterowd in referring to them as "discovery procedures," for, indeed, that is what they are.

## Intuitive Approaches

*Brainstorming.* A discovery procedure that is largely unstructured, brainstorming encourages the writer to write down anything that comes to mind about the topic, no matter how peculiar the ideas might be. Brainstorming can be done either with pencil and paper or on a computer, if a student is comfortable using it. After the student brainstorms a topic, the writing center instructor can go over the list, looking for patterns and directions for developing the paper. There are also several ways in which brainstorming can be used in a more structured way. After the student lists as many possibilities as possible, have him or her make lists of opposites and alternatives. For example, in the paper concerned with the cartoon strip, "Cathy," the student may have written "Cathy and her relationships with men." Thinking in terms of opposites the student could then write "Cathy and her relationships with women" leading to exploration of the topic "Cathy's different faces."

Brainstorming can also be done in conjunction with *clustering*, a procedure in which key ideas are circled, which then suggest other ideas to make up the cluster. For instance, in the paper concerned with "Cathy," a key idea might be "Cathy as confused feminist." Several related ideas might be "Cathy and her career," "Cathy and her boyfriend," or "Cathy and her figure." Once these key ideas are written down, then several related ideas could be generated, such as "Cathy and romance," which might be considered a subcluster of "Cathy and her boyfriend." (See below)

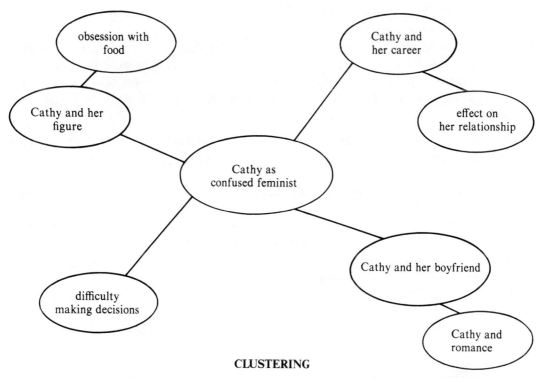

**CLUSTERING**

*Freewriting.* A technique advocated by Peter Elbow and Ken Macrorie, freewriting allows students to get their thoughts onto the page without worrying about appropriateness or correctness. It is a means of exploring an idea, sometimes enabling student to move in directions they never would have though of. Peter Elbow explains freewriting as follows:

> The idea is simply to write for ten minutes. . . . Don't stop for anything. Go quickly without rushing. Never stop to look back, to cross something out, to wonder how to spell something, to wonder what word or thought to use, to think about what you are doing. If you can't think of a word or a spelling, just use a squiggle or else write, "I can't think of it." The easiest thing is just to put down whatever is in your mind." (3)

The important point to remember about freewriting is that the student must write fast enough to use his own language, without worrying about being judged. Freewriting, like brainstorming, can also be done easily on a computer.

## Intellectual Approaches

*The Journalistic Questions.* One of the most well-known discovery procedures is the journalistic series of questions "Who? What? Where? When? Why? and

How?" Each of these questions should be answered as completely as possible, in order to generate a maximum of possibilities for writing. For instance, on the assignment based on "Cathy," it is not enough simply to answer the question "Who" with the one-word response, "Cathy." Instead, it is more effective to talk about the various personalities Cathy has, depending on who she is with—romantic self with Irving, liberated self with her mother, anxiety ridden self with her friends.

*The Pentad.* Similar to the journalistic questions, Kenneth Burke's "Pentad" asks students to explore topics through the following five categories:

**Act:** What was done? (Cathy couldn't stick to her diet and ate everything in the refrigerator)

**Agent:** Who did it? (Cathy—who longs to be slim and glamorous, yet who also wants to be taken seriously as a career person.)

**Agency:** By what means or with what was it done? (with loads of food—sweets, cookies, ice-cream—all associated with nourishment.)

**Scene:** Where and when was it done? (In the kitchen, after a fight with her boyfriend)

**Purpose:** Why was it done? (as an expression of disgust with her own weakness and with the whole obsession.)

The Pentad is useful for analyzing actions that occur in literature, a play, a movie, short story or novel, or comic strip. This discovery procedure can also yield twenty ratios, by considering any one term from the standpoints of all the others. For instance, you might consider Agent (in our example, Cathy) from the standpoint of the other four terms?

*agent-scene:* What does the scene reveal about Cathy?

*agent-agency:* What does the comic strip format reveal about Cathy?

*agent-act:* What does the situation depicted in the strip reveal about Cathy?

*agent-purpose:* What do Cathy's motives reveal about her? What is the cartoonist trying to say?

Answering Discovery Questions. Blum, Brinkman, Hoffman and Peck suggest that students ask themselves a series of "discovery questions" to generate material for papers. The questions they suggest are as follows:

What can you *describe* about your topic?

What *changes* have occurred in it?

Can you relate an *incident* about it?

What do you *remember* about it?

What are its *parts, sections,* or *elements*?

Can you give *instructions* for making or doing it?

How do you *respond* or *feel* about it?

Why is it *valuable* or *important*?

What *causes* it?

What *results* from it?

Can you clarify it by comparing it to something?

Are you *for* or *against* it? Why?

They then suggest that the student scan the responses to these to determine which ideas might be developed into a paper.

In helping students who come to the writing center with generating material for their papers, then, the instructor should:

Encourage an atmosphere of freedom and experimentation,

Help students understand that discovery of a main topic, topic or subtopic can occur at any stage of the writing process,

Have students talk about their topics before they write,

Encourage students to do *something* before they write (fill out a sheet, brainstorm, freewrite, use a discovery procedure).

Students will be grateful and will develop ideas they can really use.

## For Further Exploration

A student has come into the writing center with the assignment listed below. He says that he is not sure what the assignment requires and feels that he is stuck. Using a technique for interpreting assignments and generating ideas discussed in this chapter, write a dialogue between yourself and the student to help him get started.

_____ **Writing Assignment** _____

*In* State of the World, *biologist Thomas Lovejoy, Assistant Secretary for External Affairs of the Smithsonian Institution, is quoted as saying: "I am utterly convinced that most of the great environmental struggles will be either won or lost in the 1990's. And that by the next century it will be too late." Scientists, politicians, environmental activists, and concerned citizens have become increasingly alarmed at the rapid deterioration of the environment, and the news media now covers environmental problems on an almost daily basis.*

*Although many solutions are offered, there seems to be little consensus on how to take the steps necessary to prevent environmental disaster.*

*In a well-organized essay, address the following question:*

**How Can Individuals and Societies Effectively Respond to the Environmental Crisis Before It is "Too Late."**

*In examining how individuals and societies can respond to the environmental crisis, you will want to focus your analysis by referring to specific environmental issues.*

# THINKING ABOUT YOUR ASSIGNMENT

1.  Assignment Specifications:
    This paper should be _____ pages long. This paper is due _____ (date)

2.  Key Terms in the Assignment
    List the key terms in the assignment that give directions.

    _____

    Do any of these terms need to be defined in the paper?

    _____

3.  Does this assignment require me to develop a relationship between ideas?
    If so, which ideas must be connected?

    _____

4.  Does this assignment require me to acknowledge complexity?
    If so, list two opposing views on this topic.

    _____

    _____

5.  Does this assignment require me to consider questions of degree or make a judgment (does it say "to what extent," for example)? Must this be defined?

    _____

6.  Who is my audience? What sort of knowledge of the topic do I assume my audience has?

    _____

    Before my audience reads this paper, they think_____
    about this topic.

    After my audience reads this paper, they will think_____
    about this topic.

7.  A possible thesis or main point for this paper might be_____.

# Works Cited

Adams, James. *Conceptual Blockbusting,* second edition. New York: W. W. Norton and Company, 1979.

Belanoff, Pat, Peter Elbow, and Sheryl Fontain. *Nothing Begins With "N": New Investigations of Free Writing.* Carbondale, Illinois: Southern Illinois Press, 1991.

Blum, Jack, Carolyn Brinkman, Elizabeth Hoffman, and David Peck. *A Guide to the Whole Writing Process.* Boston: Houghton Mifflin, 1984.

Elbow, Peter. *Writing Without Teachers.* New York: Oxford University Press, 1973.

Emig, Janet. "The Composing Process: Review of the Literature." *Contemporary Rhetoric: A Conceptual Background With Readings.* Ed. W. Ross Winterowd. New York: Harcourt Brace Javanovich, 1975.

Hayes-Roth, Barbara and Frederick Hayes-Roth. "A Cognitive Model of Planning." *Cognitive Science.* 3 (1979):275–310.

Flower, Linda and John R. Hayes. *A Process Model of Composition.* Technical Report No. 1, Document Design Project. Carnegie Mellon University, 1979.

Johnson, Sabina Thorne. "The Ant and the Grasshopper: Some Reflections on Prewriting." *College English* 43 (March 1981): 232–242.

Kennedy, George E. "The Nature and Quality of Compensatory Oral Expression and its Effect on Writing in Students of College Composition." *Report to the National Institute of Education.* Washington State University, 1983.

LeFevre. Karen Burke. *Invention as a Social Act.* Carbondale, Illinois: Southern Illinois University Press, 1987.

Mack, Karin and Skejei, Eric. *Overcoming Writing Blocks.* Los Angeles: J. B. Tarcher, 1979.

Rose, Mike. *Writer's Block: The Cognitive Dimension.* Carbondate and Edwardsville: Southern Illinois University Press, 1984.

Young, Richard. "Invention: A Topographical Survey. In *Teaching Composition: Ten Bibliographical Essays.* Ed. Gary Tate. Fort Worth: Texas Christian University Press, 1976.

Zoeller, Robert, "Talk-Write: A Behavioral Pedagogy For Composition." College English 30 (January 1969):267–320.

# Chapter Five

# Working With Texts: Focusing on Purpose and Audience

A long time ago, when I was in elementary school, all the young women in the eighth grade were required to take a sewing class, in order to make their own graduation dresses. So every Tuesday and Thursday afternoons, a bunch of very silly and generally incompetent young girls would sit in Mrs. Prestopino's sewing room, diligently working on our creations. Naturally, some of us were better seamstresses than were others, and so, of course, the rate at which we worked and the kinds of mistakes we made varied considerably among us.

Mrs. Prestopino was able to cope with these differences, though, because she was a wise woman with some extremely sound pedagogical principles. Rather than requiring every girl to work on the same task at the same rate, she sensibly allowed full scope for individual differences. Serenely, Mrs. Prestopino would sit at her big sewing table at the front of the room, seemingly undisturbed by girlish chattering or the whirr of the machines. However, when any girl ran into a problem or needed instruction in the next stage of dressmaking, Mrs. Prestopino would summon the girl to her table and give her the necessary help.

Possessing neither skill, nor patience for sewing, I was a frequent visitor to Mrs. Prestopino's large table, and I know that she always adhered to the following principles of instruction:

1.  Her assignment of a particular task was based on an informed view of how one actually makes a dress.

2.  She always focused on one task at a time.

These principles are directly applicable to the concept of focusing instruction in a writing center conference. That is,

1.  Students should focus on global areas of a text, in particular, the concepts of **purpose** and **audience,** before they address surface problems, and

2.  Interchanges between tutors and students should concentrate on one or two aspects of a text. Neither tutors nor students should expect that the text will be "perfect" after only one or two visits to the writing center.

Certainly, the garment I was attempting to make needed a great deal of work (actually, I must confess that despite Mrs. Prestopino's wisdom, it *never* looked particularly good). But each time I approached her table, Mrs. Prestopino instructed me in only one facet of the sewing process at a time. She did not begin at the top of the dress and work her way down. Instead, she worked with one central problem, mentioning others only after I was ready to master them.

Good writing center tutors, then, like Mrs. Prestopino, are skilled diagnosticians and are aware of all the areas needing work in a student paper. But they have an overall concept of how texts are created and work with the student on

only one facet of the writing process at a time, focusing on others only when t. student is ready.

I have compared the effective writing center tutor to Mrs. Prestopino, the capable and intelligent sewing teacher I knew many years ago. Similarly, Donald Murray, well-known teacher, theorist, and writer, conceives of the effective writing "teacher" in the role of a physician. Murray says:

> When an accident victim is carried into the hospital emergency ward, the doctor does not start treating the patient at the top and slowly work down without a sense of priority, spending a great deal of time on the black eye before he gets to the punctured lung. Yet that is what the English teacher too often does. (19)

Murray emphasizes that the writing teacher (and this refers equally well to the writing center tutor) "should be able to spot the most critical problem in each student's writing to give that student a prescription which will be effective for him" (19). In fact, Murray points out,

> If you look at a paper covered in red . . . you will usually find that twelve or fifteen of the problems are really symptoms of one problem. A student, for example, who has not given order to his views, who is illogical in his structure, will run into all sorts of problems in syntax. Confused and complex syntax usually is an attempt to fit information in where it doesn't belong. . . . The good diagnostician will know he did not have a problem in grammar, although he was writing ungrammatically; he had a problem in thinking because he was not thinking logically. (19)

What the writing center tutor must keep in mind, then, is that it is neither possible nor desirable to discuss every aspect of a student paper in only one conference session. Although student papers often contain a bewildering array of problems and errors, constraints of time and attention make it necessary for a writing center tutor to select only one or two areas for discussion during a conference and then to choose a sequence for further instruction. It is extremely important, then for tutors to be aware of this necessity and that they base their decisions on a carefully considered and informed concept of what constitutes good composition instruction.

## Becoming Involved with the Text

When writing center tutors work on a regular basis with a consistent group of students, they get to know the students and their work and thus can diagnose papers and help students select an appropriate approach for revision with relative ease. Sometimes, in fact, they have been working with students on a particular paper from the time it had been assigned, so they are quite familiar with it. However, frequently students drop into the writing center with a completed first draft which tutors must address without having any previous knowledge of the topic, the assignment, or the student. To do this, tutors must find a way to become **involved** with the text, that is, to develop strategies of getting into it efficiently and effectively so that they can understand its strengths and weaknesses. In general, you can get involved with a text by reading part of it, asking questions about it, or reading it through, either silently or aloud.

## Getting Involved with the Text <u>Without</u> Reading It Through

You don't have to read a text from beginning to end in order to get involved with it or in order to work with a student. Sometimes, in fact, you can focus on the text more efficiently if you *don't* spend a lot of time reading it, but instead ask questions to get a sense of what the student might wish to work on. Here are a few possibilities:

1. Ask to see the assignment and ask questions about its requirements. Since you may presume that the student knows more about the assignment than you do, ask the student to explain its purpose. Ask why that purpose is important or why it matters.

2. Ask the student how the paper is likely to affect its readers, how it is likely to change readers' minds or opinions about the topic. One way to focus attention on audience is to have the student write responses to the following questions:

   Before they read my paper, my readers think _____ about my topic.

   After they read my paper, my readers will think _____ about my topic.

3. Ask the student to point out the main point or thesis and begin discussion from there.

4. Ask the student what he or she would like to work on or what he or she likes or doesn't like about the text.

5. Read the first two paragraphs and the conclusion to get a sense of the paper.

## Getting Involved with the Text by Reading It

If a student's paper is not too long, many tutors prefer to read it through completely. Some like to read it aloud or hear it read aloud. Others prefer to read it silently. I find reading aloud extremely helpful as it gives me an oral, as well as a written, sense of the text. I also find it useful when students read aloud, as they can then detect weaknesses that they might miss when they read silently. However, some students feel very uncomfortable about reading aloud, and you should not insist that they do so.

If you choose to read the text silently, it is a good idea to give the student something purposeful to do, so that he or she will not just sit there looking around the room. One suggestion that is often useful is to have the student write down what he or she perceives as the main point of the paper and then list ideas that support it. These kinds of written responses can often serve as a springboard for discussion and can focus students' attention on the overall purpose of the text. Another suggestion is to have students fill out the "Student Focus Worksheet" presented at the end of this chapter.

No matter how you choose to get involved with the text, though, be sure to begin the conference by praising *something* in the paper. A friendly, supportive remark can do a great deal toward putting students at ease and giving them a sense of confidence. If you can't think of anything in the text itself to praise, you might express enthusiasm for the topic or indicate appreciation for the student's hard work.

## Focusing on Global Areas of Text

Once you have become involved with the text, you must select an area for revision, and the most sensible approach is to begin with broad, global aspects of text—thesis, purpose, audience, structure—rather than with sentence level error or infelicities of style (after all, there is no point revising sentences that might ultimately be eliminated should the paper be refocused). To explore several possibilities for focusing a conference around global areas of text, I will use a paper you examined earlier, Jason's paper about the influence of the electronic media on society. For your convenience, here is a copy of the assignment and the paper:

## Writing Topic

*There is no question that the electronic media—T.V., radio, movies—have profoundly influenced society in the twentieth century. The media have been seen as factors in everything from the creation of designer jeans to the election of the American president. Because of their influence, the electronic media have generated a great deal of debate regarding their potential for both good and evil.*

*In a well-written essay, address the following question:*

> **Has the Influence of the Electronic Media Been Harmful to Society? Why or Why Not?**

*In your response, you should focus on specific ways the media have influenced society. You may wish to consider one or two of the following issues: myths and illusions created by the media, racial and sexual stereotypes, consumerism, social values, political values, the depiction of crime and violence. However, you are not limited to these choices and are encouraged to select your own.*

--------------------------------- **Student Essay** ---------------------------------

Television sets are on in millions of homes across the United States an average of 12 hours a day. Television has become the major source of information. After all, why read when you can sit back, relax, and watch television. Americans receive information about everything from world affairs to problems in America alone to what is happening in their community. The problem is, though, that the electronic media has tended to promote stereotypes, especially about families, minorities, and sexual values. Thus, I would say that the electronic media has harmed rather than helped society.

Television has created the illusion that the nuclear family is alive and well. Situation comedies such as The Cosby Show, Family Ties, and Growing Pains portray a happy nuclear family. Every week problems are overcome. In one episode of Growing Pains, Mike, the son, is offered drugs. He, of course, refuses and all is well as his parents praise him and tell him how proud they are of him because he did not give in to peer pressure. However, in reality, peer pressure is very strong. However, this is not the only illusion. The nuclear family is not alive because families are no longer together since half of all marriages end up in divorce. The nuclear family is not the exception rather that the rule.

All kinds of racial stereotypes are enforced by the electronic media. Japanese are shown as having oily, stringy, black hair, wearing glasses, and speaking funny. Gung Ho, a situation comedy, does exactly this. Gung Ho is about a Japanese company taking over a dead American automobile factory. And every week the Japanese are ridiculed and made fun of as the smart Caucasians play tricks. Blacks and Hispanics are perceived to have no education, no jobs and are supposed to live a life of crime. In detective shows such as Spencer, the main character who is white helps fight crime every week. He puts countless numbers of blacks in jail. Whites are shown almost always in white collar jobs. In LA Law, every one is Caucasian. In 227, the black father is a construction worker. Homosexuals are also shown as people apart from the human race. In Three's Company, Jack pretends to be gay in order to live with his two female roommates. So, in front of the manager he always acts feminine.

Commercials on television also send messages to young girls that they must be beautiful, thin, and have a great body. The California girl is in. Pringles potato chips has beautiful girls lying by the pool eating their product. The guys must also be good looking but to a lesser degree. What men have to be is rich in order to get the girl.

Unless the electronic media changes its programming drastically, all of these stereotypes will continue to be seen by countless viewers. Television affects the way we perceive different things and so far it has not done an accurate job.

# Working with Jason's Paper in the Writing Center

There are several approaches a tutor might take with such a paper, and, indeed, there is no one way to work with Jason on this paper. But first, let us look at an approach that is *unlikely* to be effective:

**Tutor:** Why don't you read the first paragraph aloud to me.
**Jason:** (reads paper aloud) I think I have begun both the first and second sentences with the work "television." I should probably change one of them.
**Tutor:** Very good. Now how about the last two sentences in the paragraph. You use the phrase "electronic media" twice as well.

In the above interchange, the writing center tutor and Jason simply read the paper through, the tutor pointing out errors as they occurred. Moreover, instead of formulating an approach to the text as a whole, the writing center tutor directed Jason simply to work through some of the repetitive diction in the opening paragraph, without exploring if the sentences in that paragraph are really relevant to the overall thesis of the paper. In fact, it is quite possible that some of the material in the opening paragraph may have to be deleted once the paper is refocused and reorganized, so this discussion about diction wasted the time of both tutor and student. Moreover, in this interchange, the tutor gave Jason the false impression that he should pay attention to diction before he has clarified his thesis and organizational structure. Such a sequence is likely to prevent Jason from developing his ideas properly, in that he will be inhibited by this disproportionate concentration on surface detail.

Unfortunately, an almost fanatic concern with surface correctness has characterized composition teaching for the past twenty-five years, a concern that you might recognize from your own school background. As Erika Lindemann points out, "for generations, most English teachers have given first priority to correct usage. . . . All writers disagree with this emphasis. Language should be used correctly, but the final careful editing cannot take place until the writer has discovered, by writing, what he has to say and how he wants to say it" (105).

Moreover, many students, too, conceive of revision solely in terms of changing the "words." Nancy Sommers' study of revision strategies of student writers and experienced adult writers suggest that "students understand the revision process as a rewording activity. . . . The students place a symbolic importance on their selection and rejection of words as the determiners of success or failure for their compositions. When revising, they primarily ask themselves: Can I find a better word or phrase?"(381). Sommers points out that although the students did not see revision as an activity for the development or modification of ideas, that the adult writers conceived of revising as "finding the form and shaper of their argument" (384). After a concern for form, the experienced writers indicated a second objective—a concern for their readership. They did not deal with external facets of their papers until their paper was in relatively final form.

In general, then, it is best not to work on surface difficulties in a student paper before helping the student focus a topic, develop a thesis, and construct an organizational scheme. Help students understand that writing is primarily concerned with communicating an idea to an audience and that often writers do not really clarify their ideas until they have rewritten the paper many times, adding, deleting, substituting, and rearranging. Urge students to save the proofreading and editing until a later time.

I should point out, though, that there may be a few instances when you would choose to begin with a relatively minor writing difficult, even if the paper under consideration also needed more substantial revision. Sometimes a student is referred to the writing center by an instructor who is planning to deal with structural revision in the classroom and who, therefore, has assigned a specific surface skill for the student to learn on his or her own. Or perhaps you may choose to begin working with a particular student on a surface area of writing simply because it is a more manageable task for the student to complete, one that will provide the student with an immediate feeling of achievement. Many students come to a writing center having experienced a great deal of frustration associated with writing. For such students, it might be psychologically advantageous to be assigned to work on an easily learned skill, such as comma placement, rather than be confronted with the more difficult and time consuming undertaking of focusing a thesis or restructuring the paper as a whole.

Generally, however, it is better to begin with the global issues of writing and to save surface editing for a later time. As Murray points out, a writing teacher (or a writing center tutor) "is not trying to identify and correct every fault in a paper; he is not trying to cover every point in a conference. He is trying to find one central problem on each paper and prescribe a treatment" (20).

# Focusing Instruction Through Purpose

An approach that I have found extremely useful in focusing a writing center conference is to direct student attention to the purpose of the paper (that is, begin by asking the student why he or she is writing this paper). At first, students may quip that they are writing the paper to pass a course or to please a teacher. However, this is an important question for you to ask and for students to ask themselves whenever they write, as it focuses attention on overall structure and development. Here are some ideas to help students focus their attention on the idea of purpose:

1. Ask students, "what important point does your paper make? Can you point to a sentence or section in the paper where that point is established?"

2. Have students complete this sentence:

   The purpose of my paper is to prove (show, establish) _____. (The student can complete this sentence while you are reading the paper.)

3. To focus attention on the relationship between purpose and audience, have students complete these sentences:

   Before my readers read my paper, they think _____ about the topic.
   After my readers read my paper, they will think _____ about the topic.

4. Ask students *why* their point is important (this is the "so-what" approach).

Here is an example of a conference in which tutor Bill challenges Jason to think about the purpose and point of his paper.

**Bill:** Well, you certainly have used a lot of examples in this paper. You discuss some really important points.

**Jason:** You mean its perfect just as it is?

**Bill:** Not exactly. I can see that you showed that these programs are completely unrealistic. You say that they show that problems can be solved easily and that they give the impression that the nuclear family is still very common. You also talk about stereotypes.

**Jason:** Right. That was the assignment.

**Bill:** Well, let's go back to the assignment for a minute. What was it again that you were supposed to write about?

**Jason:** (reads) "Has the electronic media been harmful to society?" Yeah, that's right. That's my thesis. Right there at the end of the first paragraph. I say it right there that I think its been harmful.

**Bill:** That's right. You do. But then—okay, let's look at the first paragraph after the introduction. Right here. What do you talk about in this paragraph?

**Jason:** I, um, talk about the nuclear family not being the norm anymore. Oh—and I talk about problems being solved easily—like turning down drugs.

**Bill:** Yeah, that's right. And you say that these programs are not too realistic.

**Jason:** Yeah. That's right. I mean, its a joke, a real fantasy—completely out of this world.

**Bill:** Well, I have to agree with you. But so what? So what if these programs are unrealistic? Does that matter?

**Jason:** Wait a minute. I'm not sure what you mean.

**Bill:** Okay. Lots of shows are unrealistic, and I bet you even watch some of them. Did you ever see Mickey Mouse? What's wrong with a show being unrealistic?

**Jason:** Well, its no problem if the shows are *supposed* to be unrealistic, like Mickey Mouse, and everyone knows that. But some of the people who watch these shows, like—well—kids especially, may think they're real, or get weird ideas about how life is from these shows. And—like—lots of people's families don't have lives like they show on t.v. So people who watch may feel bad that . . . well, like that their own families are not like those on t.v. And with the drug thing, well, it gives the viewer the idea that drugs are no big deal. Just say "no" quickly and everything will be fine. That's not the way it is, especially for some people, like those who live in the ghetto.

**Bill:** Hey, that's good. That's the sort of stuff that ought to be in the paper.

**Jason:** Oh. So I ought to explain why these shows are bad.

**Bill:** Yes. I think that would improve the paper a lot. And it would also create a tighter connection between your thesis about the harm that t.v. can cause and the examples you have in your paper. I mean, if someone tells me that t.v. gives people unrealistic ideas about what families are like and makes big problems seem like nothing, I can't just say "so what," can I?

**Jason:** I can do the same thing with the stereotypes, right?

**Bill:** Right. That's good. In fact your discussion of the stereotypes might really be expanded with this kind of approach. I'll be interested to see the kind of analysis you do. The paper is going to be a lot more developed and tied together once you make a few connections.

In this interchange, Bill's provocative question "so what" challenged Jason into thinking about the impact of his paper and into making connections between his thesis statement and the examples he cites. Perhaps, once he begins developing these connections, his paper will have a more coherent focus.

## Focusing Instruction Through Audience

A related approach to working with a text is to view it in terms of audience, that is, to direct students' attention to the impact that the paper is likely to have on its readers. A useful way to accomplish this is for the writing center tutor to assume the role of the audience, providing feedback to the student about what the paper is communicating to the reader. For example, in discussing Jason's paper, you might indicate to Jason that you are getting a bit confused since he is talking about so many different problems with television and that you might need further expansion of one or two of them. Or you might say something like, "Oh I was expecting you to talk about how society has been harmed. But you are showing me that these programs are unrealistic." Or you might say, "After reading your paper, I get the idea that many of these shows are unrealistic. What's wrong with an unrealistic show?" Such questions might generate thinking about the effects of lack of realism and stereotypical depictions of minorities and might then suggest to Jason that he further explore the topic rather than simply list examples.

Playing the part of the audience can help students realize that what they may have intended to say may not actually be written in their early drafts, a problem experienced by all writers at one time or another. As was discussed earlier, beginning writers, in particular, often produce "writer-based prose," characterized by gaps in logic or sketchily presented events. Consider, for example, the following paragraph:

> Sometimes my angry feelings explode inside of me. Last night, for instance, I rushed out of the house, jumped into my car, and raced up this hill near my house. I tore the paper out of my notebook and ripped it into a thousand pieces. I felt a lot better after that. But later on, when I had to have my car towed down the hill, I wondered if it had been worth it.

In this excerpt, there are several missing pieces of information. Why was the student so angry? What did the paper have to do with it (had it been given a failing grade?) Why did the car have to be towed? It seems as if the student wrote this draft under the impression that the audience was thoroughly familiar with the situation.

Writing center tutors can help students become aware of when they have written "writer-based prose." Comments such as "Wait. I didn't understand that section," or "What do you mean by that?" help students realize which sections of a text might require additional clarification or discussion. As James Moffet says in *Teaching the Universe of Discourse*, "writing mistakes are not made in ignorance of common sense requirements; they are made for other reasons that advice cannot prevent. Usually, the student thinks he has made a logical transition in a narrative point, which means . . . he is deceived by his own egocentricity. What he needs is not rules but awareness" (202).

Approaching a writing center conference by focusing on audience is also useful when a student paper expresses an offensive or unexamined viewpoint. Sometimes students don't realize that their views may be biased or sexist; they are completely unaware that their papers could be offensive to their readers. In such cases, I suggest that tutors not become personally involved with the position expressed and not get angry (even if it is tempting to do so). Instead, work with the student to imagine how the text is likely to affect its audience. Remind the student that the aim of a text is to convince an audience of a position or at least to move an audience to change its mind about a topic; therefore, an outrageous or unsupported view is not likely to be successful.

# Approaching Instruction Through Narrowing and Focusing the Topic

A common problem students bring to the writing center is that of overly broad, unfocused topics, and a useful way to spend a writing center conference is to work on narrowing and focusing. First, let's define these terms. What is the difference between "narrowing" and "focusing?"

Richard Coe maintains that *narrowing* limits a writer to a part of the original topic. "It is equivalent to what a photographer does by zooming in with a zoom lens (or switching to a long lens). The name of the photograph becomes smaller, the outer boundaries of the topic are reduced" (272). Thus, when one focuses a topic, the broad subject "world peace" might become "Peace in the Philippines," or "The Literacy Crisis" might become "The Literacy Crisis in Los Angeles." Usually, the narrowing of a topic is determined by a real division in the subject matter.

*Focusing*, according to Coe, limits a writer to a particular aspect of the original topic. This restriction is determined largely by how the writer looks at the topic, equivalent to what a photographer does by adjusting focal length. "The frame of the picture or outer boundaries of the writing topic remain the same, but distinct aspects come into sharp focus and receive emphasis" (273). Thus, "Peace in the Philippines" might become "What are the Obstacles to Peace in the Philippines?" "The Literacy Crisis in Los Angeles?" might become "What are the Causes of the Literary Crisis in Los Angeles?" Jason's paper, which is concerned with various harmful effects of the electronic media, might be more narrowly focused around how television promotes racial stereotypes.

## Focusing the Thesis Through the Topic-Problem-Thesis Method

Linda Flower suggests that a good method of focusing a thesis is to move from topic to problem to thesis. For instance, if the topic is simply "required courses in college," the student might write a simple description of existing required courses, a paper which would be likely to have only limited use, since students could probably get the same information more concisely from the college catalogue. Many students, though, are unable to focus a topic other than through classification and description, because they do not view writing as a problem solving technique or as a means of accomplishing a specific purpose. Flower's method of coming up with a workable thesis, however, advises students to ask themselves whether the general topic contains some problematic issue, around which to build an idea. The following interchange, for example, could be used to help students focus a thesis by becoming aware of a problem within the general topic:

**Student:** The topic is pretty general. Required courses in college. So all I could think of doing was writing a description of the required courses we all have to take here. It's a pretty boring idea.

**Tutor:** Well, I don't know if it's boring. But I do wonder why anyone would be interested in reading a paper on that topic. After all, everyone knows that required courses are really important and that every student is absolutely thrilled about having to take them.

**Student:** Right. Big joke! Students usually *hate* required courses. Like this writing course, for instance. Do you think I would be taking this course, if I didn't have to?

**Tutor:** Well, would you?

**Student:** Actually, I'm not sure. Most of the time I might say, "not on your life." But on the other hand, I guess I really believe that I should know how to write when I go into the Business world. Yeah, I guess I would take the course. And probably my computer course, too.

**Tutor:** Do you think other students feel as you do?

**Student:** I don't know. All they ever do is complain about all the general education courses they have to take. Maybe they don't think about it much.

**Tutor:** It seems, then, as if there exists a problem within this general topic "required courses on campus." Can you see what the problem is?

**Student:** Well, yeah, I think so. Students complain all the time about having to take all these requirements. Yet these requirements, at least some of them, are really important for them to have. And a lot of students don't understand that.

**Tutor:** Great! Then let's assume that you are writing this paper about required courses for an audience of students. What might you say that would have some interest to them?

**Student:** I might try to show them how these required courses are really necessary for them in the long run. They might then stop complaining so much about having to take them.

**Tutor:** Do you think, then, that all required courses are necessary?

**Student:** Well, probably not all of them. I sure can't see the point of that poetry class. Maybe I should say that students should be shown the reasons certain courses are required. Then they might understand better.

**Tutor:** Good. That's a real thesis with a real point. Now let's recall again how you came up with it, so that you might be able to do it again on a next paper. You started with the general topic "Required courses on campus." Then you started to think about a problem within the topic—

**Student:** Like the problem of how students hate required courses.

**Tutor:** Right! Then you developed a thesis which addressed that problem. That's the method to remember: Go from topic to problem to thesis. It's a method you can use with a variety of topics.

Using the "Topic→Problem→Thesis" method is a useful, transferable strategy which students can practice, even when they don't actually write the paper. Simply present students with a list of possible, fairly general topics and ask them to find a problem within each of them. Then, focusing on a specific audience, they might try formulating a thesis which deals with the problem within the general topic.

Another strategy that helps students focus a thesis is to have them set specific goals for the paper to accomplish, what they wish readers to do or think after they have read the paper (this strategy is, of course, similar to the two questions cited earlier in this chapter). For instance, if the topic is "Problems with College Roommates," a simple *topic* based plan would be concerned only with a list of problems college students have with their roommates, a topic which might be of mild interest, particular if it were written humorously, but would not be of general concern.

However, a *goal* based plan would be concerned with showing a readership of college students how problems with roommates can affect performance in classes and how one can minimize such problems with insight and planning. The *topic* based plan is concerned only with a presentation of the topic. The *goal* based plan presupposes that effective prose can generate action and can have important consequences. Thus, students can learn to focus their theses by considering what goals they wish their papers to accomplish.

# Fostering Further Development:
# Returning to Idea Generation

Finding a new focus for a paper often means selecting one aspect of a draft and working with prewriting techniques in order to develop it. Jason's paper, like those of many students, lists a number of ideas without developing them fully—the unrealistic portrayal of family life, the depiction of social problems as easy to solve, the promotion of racial, ethnic, and gender stereotypes. This *Laundry List* approach means that no topic can be discussed adequately—the student mentions something and then moves on to something else. To focus and develop his paper, Jason might do some brainstorming or clustering on one aspect of his paper, the promotion of stereotypes, for example. As Jason develops additional material on this topic, his focus might then change, and he might decide to devote his whole paper to this one aspect of the topic.

Keep in mind, though, when working with students to develop one aspect of a topic and perhaps to eliminate unrelated material, that students often hate to drop anything they have written. They recall how much work it was for them to write those sections and often feel that everything they have written should be included—*nothing* should be wasted, even if it is slightly off topic. Thus, decisions to eliminate anything should always be made by students, themselves. Usually, once students see that they have generated additional material and that they are able to probe a topic more deeply because of this additional focus, they will be more inclined to detach themselves from pieces of their writing and perhaps save them for another paper.

When working with texts in the writing center, then, the following principles apply:

1. The focus of a writing center conference should be *chosen* deliberately. Paper diagnosis and work on revision should not be done haphazardly.
2. The focus of a writing center conference should be based on an informed view of the writing process.
3. In general, global areas of discourse should be discussed before surface problems.
4. During a writing center conference, it is best to discuss one or two concepts at a time. Don't overwhelm the student by trying to cover everything in one conference.

## Exercise

A student has come into the writing center with a rough draft that was written in response to the assignment below. Read the assignment and the student paper. Then fill out the form marked "Conference Format Worksheet." After you have completed this, work with a partner or in a small group comparing your responses.

## _____ Assignment: Police and the Use of Force _____

### Background

*On March 3, 1991, Los Angeles Police Department officers and California Highway Patrol Officers allegedly gave chase to a suspect vehicle that refused to stop. When the car was halted, officers pulled the driver, Rodney King, from the car and began pummeling him with kicks and nightstick blows. The officers were unaware that the incident was being videotaped by a neighbor. Since the tape has come to light, a nationwide public outcry against the violence has been directed at the LAPD and its chief, Daryl Gates.*

*This incident focuses new and closer scrutiny upon the role of police officers and the powers they wield while on duty serving the public good. The King incident, while unusually controversial, represents merely one of thousands of allegations of police brutality leveled at police departments in cities throughout America.*

## Assignment

*Think about the topic of police use of force (not only on the King incident) and respond to one of the following three questions:*

1. *If we grant that officers must sometimes use force in policing actions, where and how should the line be drawn between acceptable and unacceptable levels of force?*
2. *What can be done to prevent police brutality?*
3. *What does the increasing number of reported police brutality cases indicate about our society?*

---
### Student Paper
---

### Stepping Into a Cop's Shoes

The city, and the nation are in an uproar. For one of the few times in history, the actions of a group of bad cops have been caught of film. Most people know about the violence that goes on in the streets; the drugs, the theft, the killing, at last according to a *Newsweek* poll, yet all of it is part of living in a metropolis such as Los Angeles. For the most part, people have come to accept the fact that police brutality does exist, but those on the receiving end "deserve it." This time, though, through the wonder of modern video technology, the malicious beating of a suspect has been captured on videocassette. The situation is intense, especially for an already controversial police superintendant who has been known in the past to make racial slurs. Especially for a police department that already has a reputation for employing a slew of "bad cops," causing their reputation to plummet even further. For Rodney King, this incident will probably be reflected in his face and in his speech for the rest of his life. For officers Koon, Wind, Powell, and Briseno, it will be reflected on their records and perpetuated in their daily lives for the rest of their careers, probably not in the law enforcement field. For the members of the Los Angeles Police department, it means having to live with one hand tied behind your back, being constantly analyzed, the "fishbowl" effect as it is called. For we may all sit back in our homes and safely say "that was wrong to beat that man," but none of us would be willing to put our lives on the line, our family at stake, to make sure a child doesn't get run over by a Hundai Excel.

For members of the Los Angeles Police Department, life is a "fishbowl" now, no longer can they go out in public without being scrutinized. Everyone wonders, "is he just as bad as those cops that beat Rodney King?" For even though they did nothing wrong, they will have to live with it from now on executing their duties as police officers. The taunts of "where's my video camera?" when stopping a common smart-ass speeder will fade in time, but a scarred badge never will. For now, more swiftly than judgment was passed on Rodney King, judgment is being passed by the public.

For the past two weeks, especially in Los Angles, the public has seen the King video many, many times along with the sharp, angry words of a t.v. reporter. The mass man is quick to judge when he sees things on television, after all, that's probably how he picked who he voted for, if he voted. But all this doesn't matter to him, the perils of being a police officer, the pressure behind the job, the pressure being human is not good enough, only revenge is.

Needless to say, Joe Blow watching Rodney King getting beaten on television has never stepped in the shoes of a police officer and doesn't realize what it's like to stare down the barrel of a gun. He will never realize what it's like to approach a car you have just pulled over for speeding. Simply because Joe Blow is too much of a coward to do it himself, yet his cowardice flees when he sits in his armchair and passes judgement on a handful of cops.

The job of a police officer is a scary one, and the scariest part of that job is fear, fear of the unknown. When an officer gets out and approached a car he has pulled over, a million thoughts are racing through his mind. Thoughts such as the identity of the subject, it could be an elderly woman on her way home, it could be a serial killer leaving the scene of the crime. The typical speeder is not readily visible by the way he speeds, and just because he's driving an ordinary car such as a Hyundai Excel doesn't make him any less of a threat. Unfortunately, a cop doesn't have the foresight to see if he is dealing with a harmless speeder, or a wanted felon, its not possible.

The fact is that Rodney King broke the law. For a moment let's forget that he was brutally beaten. Even though King is a criminal, and maliciously broke the law, the actions of the four police officers were not justified. However, we cannot overlook the fact that Rodney King is a criminal, a previously convicted criminal. Rodney King eluded the police, was speeding (regardless of whether he was going 110 or 70 miles per hour, depending on whether you believe the LAPD or the CHP, respectively), he ran several red lights, he resisted arrest, he was found to have both alcohol and traces of marijuana in his bloodstream. After he was apprehended, he resisted arrest, the stun gun had no effect on him and he jumped a police officer. The policemen on the scene then took a brutal tactic too far. In this tactic, the officers surround the suspect and use all force necessary to bring him to submission. When King submitted, some veteran officers didn't stop, they continued to maliciously beat him. Some ask why the others watched. The reasons vary anywhere from just being stunned by this treatment and the inability of a rookie cop to take action or question the action of a veteran police officer.

The problem with the job of a cop is that they are forced to fight what we refuse to deal with. Those out there being arrested by the LAPD aren't idea citizens, and they don't go quietly. Week after week police officers watch their comrades go down just like Tina Kerbrat who was shot point blank in the face by a man she was going to ticket for drinking in public. How can the LAPD deal with drug dealers with uzis when they lose officers to people they try to arrest for misdemeanors? The only possible way is to be tough. A cop who is compassionate and caring out on the streets is frequently a dead cop. Unfortunately, cops are human, they have feelings and emotions and they explode. The actions of Koon, Wind, Powell, and Briseno only add fuel to the fire against them now. No it is even tougher to fight crime on the streets being under the microscope.

❖

## CONFERENCE FORMAT WORK SHEET
## PLANNING THE FOCUS AND SEQUENCE OF INSTRUCTION

*A student has come to the Writing Center with a paper based on the police brutality assignment outlined above. He knows that his paper needs some additional work, but he doesn't know what he should do. What sort of conference should you hold with this student?*

*To generate thinking on this issue, please answer the following questions. Then work in groups or in pairs to compare your answers:*

1. To improve this paper, the writer should concentrate on the following areas:

    1) _____

    2) _____

    3) _____

    4) _____

2. Which area will you concentrate on during the first conference?

3. Assuming you can get the student to return for additional conferences, what sequence of instruction will you develop? (What will you work on first, what second, etc.).

    _____

    _____

    _____

    _____

# Works Cited

Coe, Richard. "If Not to Narrow, Then How to Focus: Two Techniques for Focusing." *College Composition and Communication* 32 (October 1981): 272–278.

Flower, Linda. *Problem-Solving Strategies for Writers.* New York: Harcourt Brace Jovanovich, 1981.

Lindemann, Erika. *A Rhetoric For Writing Teachers.* New York: Oxford University Press, 1982.

Moffett, James. *Teaching the Universe of Discourse.* New York: Houghton Mifflin, 1968.

Murray, Donald. *A Writer Teaches Writing.* Boston: Houghton Mifflin, 1968.

Sommers, Nancy. "Revision Strategies of Student Writers and Experienced Adult Writers." *College Composition and Communication* 31 (December 1980):378–389.

# Chapter Six

# Working With Texts: Organization, Structure, Sentence Level Revision

In the previous chapter, I introduced Mrs. Prestopino, the sewing teacher who had a clear sense of how to help others learn, and I also mentioned Donald Murray's reference to the writing teacher's diagnostic skills as similar to those of a physician. However, although diagnosis is a crucial first step in improving a text, it must be followed by specific suggestions for revision; revision strategies ought to be part of a writing center tutor's "bag of tricks." After all, Mrs. Prestopino would not have done a good job if she had simply pointed out what was wrong with my graduation dress, without giving me instruction on how to improve it, nor would it be adequate for a physician simply to notice that I had broken my leg without recommending some form of treatment. Thus, writing center tutors should not only help students figure out what may need additional work in their papers—they should also help them learn how to do that work effectively so that they can then apply what they have learned to a subsequent writing task.

This chapter discusses strategies you can use to help students work with their texts in the writing center. It is concerned especially with helping students improve organization and structure and undertake sentence level revision.

# Helping Students Develop Organizational Strategies

Papers may be disorganized both on an overall conceptual level and/or within individual paragraphs. A paper, as a whole, may be considered "disorganized" when its main points are not grouped thematically, are not strongly linked to the main idea or thesis of the paper, or are not presented in a logical sequence. In some instances, the paper may be globally well structured, but individual paragraphs may need reorganization. These paragraphs will be characterized by sentences that are not grouped according to the ideas they express or may jump from one idea to another without adequate connection. Sometimes, of course, a paper may be disorganized in both ways.

## Helping Students Perceive Faulty Organization

When a student brings in a disorganized paper, there is a great temptation simply to seize it, point out that it is disorganized, and then reorganize it yourself. Creating structural order is a particularly satisfying task—perhaps it fulfills the same needs as reorganizing a desk or a closet. In the interest of helping students become better writers, though, resist this temptation—instead, help students *learn to recognize* that their papers are disorganized and then help them develop strategies they can use to revise.

Sometimes, when students bring their papers to the writing center and begin to reread them, they, themselves, will recognize the need for reorganization, without the tutor having to say or do anything. When this occurs, it is usually because sufficient time has elapsed since the paper was written, so that students are able to view it from a more distant perspective and will thus be able to notice problems more easily than when they are immersed in the actual writing process. It is generally known that when writers put their writing aside for a while, in fact for even a short amount of time, that they are better able to perceive what needs revision. This principle also pertains to helping students recognize faulty organization, and it means that by simply providing the opportunity for students to look over their texts, you will be helping them perceive faulty organization, without your having to do anything further.

## Faulty Organization Sometimes Means Faulty Thinking

Another point to keep in mind about faulty organization is that it is often not the primary problem with the paper—rather it may be a *symptom* of inadequate reflection—the paper is poorly organized because the student has not really clarified what it is that he or she is trying to say. It may contain a few ideas, developed with sketchy examples, but is characterized by an overall incoherence that may be viewed initially as an organizational problem. In addressing what may seem to be organizational problems in the writing center, then, it is a good idea to begin by talking to the student about the goals of the paper in relation to audience and about what the paper is supposed to accomplish. What often happens is that once the student's ideas are clarified and after the draft is revised, the organizational problems disappear by themselves.

For example, Suzanne came to the writing center with the following paper concerned with an educational reform. The assignment and the paper are reproduced below:

## Assignment

Write an essay in which you argue for a significant reform within the educational system that you have known as a student. Support your case with evidence and arguments drawn from your own experience.

_____ **Suzanne's draft** _____

### *Exams: Who Needs Them?*

The purpose of education is to gather information that will add to the existing knowledge in our minds. A method has been developed by many teachers in which they believe will help the student provide evidence of what they have learned. Their method is giving exams. We have all been faced with the pressures that proceed an upcoming exam. As a result, many students are confronted with doubts of why they have to take an exam. They also consider the question of whether or not it is fair.

We all try to avoid any kind of pressure that may overcome us. In many ways, we usually seem to get defeated by it. The knowledge of having to take an upcoming accumulative exam can exert a great amount of pressure. Having many other worries and activities to think about and to take care of, a handicap results. Many students have other pressures on them as well, many other courses to think about instead of just one. Also, some students are away from home for the first time and have to face that pressure as well. Just getting laundry done is sometimes a big pressure, especially for someone who has never done it before. So with many other engagements, time becomes limited and the hours of studying lessened. The countless minutes pass endlessly as one tries to recall all the information learned from the beginning of the year. Many are familiar with this process. It is the process of cramming. As a result, many students stay up until they think they've studied enough only to encounter that their minds have blanked out before the test because of lack of sleep and too much input of information all at once. This ineffective method makes many students feel that they are being forced to study. Many students then become reluctant to study and therefore rebel by finding no other alternative but to cheat.

To my understanding, exams, in many cases are unfair. It exerts pressure on students, creates tension between other activities and wastes time. I believe that exams are unfair because the effort put into studying throughout the year doesn't always reflect how well a person did on the exam. It may seem that a full year of hard work is wasted as a student "bombs" the exam because of unavoidable circumstances that disrupts one's ability to study or concentrate.

As one faces the trauma of exam taking, one begins to doubt the necessity of it. I don't find it a necessity to study endlessly for an exam only to find that what I have studied is not found on the test. Many times, the questions pertain to trivial details of the study and therefore result in a lower grade. It is useless to try to let so much information enter all at once only to discover that it has been forgotten within the following week. Taking an exam is unnecessary in that it is not effective in showing all that one has accomplished throughout the year, in just one test.

Others find that taking tests are necessary for a student to ingrain the knowledge into their heads. On the contrary, I believe that it is a means of easily forgetting what has been learned due to the cramming process that many students practice. Some also believe that it is a helpful way of gathering knowledge and making sense of it all. It would be more difficult, though, to make sense out of something when one is under pressure. In my opinion, exams do not determine how much knowledge a person has accumulated.

I would only agree with exam taking if the contents were focused on broad, not trivial details. I think that schools should only use the exam method only with daily or weekly quizzes. The grades on these quizzes would indicate a student's progress throughout the year. This would result in a grade rightly earned without one exam grade completely dominating. In this process, the amount of students cramming would lessen. Also, the less information there is to study, the easier it is to remember. Working on one small portion at a time would create a less pressurized method of learning.

Suzanne came to the Writing Center because she felt that her paper was "disorganized." However, when the tutor read the draft, he realized that what she perceived as "disorganization" was really a lack of sustained reflection about the subject. Before she could "reorganize" her paper, Suzanne needed to do some additional thinking about her thesis and the main points she was using to support it. Here is the conference Todd, a tutor in the writing center, had with Suzanne:

**Todd:** Okay, you have a lot of good ideas in this draft, things we can work with. But before we start, tell me what was the assignment again?

**Suzanne:** (Looking over the assignment sheet) I'm supposed to talk about a reform in the educational system and support it with my own experience.

**Todd:** Right. Okay. Now—can you summarize the reform you are arguing for.

**Suzanne:** It's here in my title. I think exams should be eliminated.

**Todd:** Okay. And can you summarize your reasons?

**Suzanne:** Well, it's like I say here. They cause a lot of pressure. And people cram for them so they don't learn anything.

**Todd:** So you think all exams should be eliminated.

**Suzanne:** Definitely. I mean, I hardly got any sleep during finals week. I was so nervous. And I ate a lot of junk food too.

**Todd:** I can relate to that. But think about this idea for a minute. You say that all exams should be eliminated, and your paper doesn't distinguish between different kinds of exams or different situations. But—how about—okay— When you go to a doctor, does he or she have a medical degree?

**Suzanne:** Of course. I wouldn't go to some quack who didn't have a degree.

**Todd:** And what does that degree mean? I mean, how do you get a medical degree?

**Suzanne:** Well, I don't know exactly, but I guess it means that the doctor took courses and passed his medical boards—stuff like that.

**Todd:** Passed his boards? Is that some kind of an exam?

**Suzanne:** Oh boy. Yeah, some kind of exam, I suppose. But, wait a minute—I think the exams doctors have to take have more to do with what they learn in their classes. Or maybe they have more to do with what they will be doing when they become doctors. You know, like practical stuff.

**Todd:** You mean that their exams are better connected to subject matter and to their work.

**Suzanne:** That's right. Oh, and maybe they have more of them, so that not everything is connected to that one final exam. It's wrong to put everything on one test. It's too much pressure. I hardly got any sleep during finals week—I really looked awful.

**Todd:** Wait—so its final exams, big exams, that you think need reform?

**Suzanne:** Well, it's like I say in my paper. Final exams cause pressure—so much pressure that people start to cram and then they don't learn anything and lose a lot of sleep. I was exhausted, I can tell you. And I don't think I learned anything either. I forgot it all right afterwards.

**Todd:** So the pressure interferes with learning?

**Suzanne:** That's right. People get crazy and just memorize for the test. Also, they don't learn anything because they forget what they studied as soon as the test is over.

**Todd:** Okay. Let's think about getting some of these ideas down on paper. Can you write down your main thesis?

**Suzanne:** (Writes) "The system of having one main final exam at the end of a course should be changed."

**Todd:** Great! Now, can you list at least two reasons for your opinion?

**Suzanne:** (Writes) "1. Final exams cause too much pressure." Hmnn, I don't know if I can think of anything else.

**Todd:** Sure you can. What did you say about learning just now?

**Suzanne:** Oh. Right. (Writes) "2. Final exams don't help students learn."

**Todd:** Terrific! Now lets look over your paper again and see how it fits these ideas.

**Suzanne:** Do you mean I have to write the whole paper over again?

**Todd:** No. Let's take this pink marker (one underline) and mark every sentence that has to do with the idea of pressure. Then lets use the blue marker (two underlines) to mark sentences that have to do with learning.

(after Todd and Suzanne went through the paper, it looked like this).

### _Exams: Who Needs Them?_

The purpose of education is to gather information that will add to the existing knowledge in our minds. A method has been developed by many teachers in which they believe will help the student provide evidence of what they have learned. Their method is giving exams. We have all been faced with the pressures that proceed an upcoming exam. As a result, many students are confronted with doubts of why they have to take an exam. They also consider the question of whether or not it is fair.

We all try to avoid any kind of pressure that may overcome us. In many ways, we usually seem to get defeated by it. The knowledge of having to take an upcoming accumulative exam can exert a great amount of pressure. Having many other worries and activities to think about and to take care of, a handicap results. Many students have other pressures on them as well, many other courses to think about instead of just one. Also, some students are away from home for the first time and have to face that pressure as well. Just getting laundry done is sometimes a big pressure, especially for someone who has never done it before. So with many other engagements, time becomes limited and the hours of studying lessened. The countless minutes pass endlessly as one tries to recall all the information learned from the beginning of the year. Many are familiar with this process. It is the process of cramming. As a result, many students stay up until they think they've studied enough only to encounter that their minds have blanked out before the test because of lack of sleep and too much input of information all at once. This ineffective method makes many students feel that they are being forced to study. Many students then become reluctant to study and therefore rebel by finding no other alternative but to cheat.

To my understanding, exams, in many cases are unfair. It exerts pressure on students, creates tension between other activities and wastes time. I believe that exams are unfair because the effort put into studying throughout the year doesn't always reflect how well a person did on the exam. It may seem that a full year of hard work is wasted as a student "bombs" the exam because of unavoidable circumstances that disrupts one's ability to study or concentrate.

As one faces the trauma of exam taking, one begins to doubt the necessity of it. I don't find it a necessity to study endlessly for an exam only to find that what I have studied is not found on the test. Many times, the questions pertain to trivial details of the study and therefore result in a lower grade. It is useless to try to let so much information enter all at once only to discover that it has been forgotten within the following week. Taking an exam is unnecessary in that it is not effective in showing all that one has accomplished throughout the year, in just one test.

Others find that taking tests are necessary for a student to ingrain the knowledge into their heads. <u>On the contrary, I believe that it is a means of easily forgetting what has been learned due to the cramming process that many students practice.</u> Some also believe that it is a helpful way of gathering knowledge and making sense of it all. <u>It would be more difficult, though, to make sense out of something when one is under pressure.</u> <u>In my opinion, exams do not determine how much knowledge a person has accumulated.</u>

I would only agree with exam taking if the contents were focused on broad, not trivial details. I think that schools should only use the exam method only with daily or weekly quizzes. The grades on these quizzes would indicate a student's progress throughout the year. This would result in a grade rightly earned without one exam grade completely dominating. In this process, the amount of students cramming would lessen. Also, the less information there is to study, the easier it is to remember. <u>Working on one small portion at a time would create a less pressurized method of learning.</u>

**Todd:** You see, when you mark the text this way, you can often find a lot of good ideas you can use. Now let's talk about grouping these ideas and also about some ideas you might have for reforming the exam system. That might be another section.

In this interchange, Todd did not immediately focus on organization because it was apparent that Suzanne needed to think more deeply about her thesis. However, once she had a few ideas, he used the system of marking sentences to locate those that could be grouped together. This is a strategy that is useful for detecting conceptual as well as sentence level disorganization.

## Detecting Faulty Organization Through Outlining and Tree Diagrams

Outlining is often regarded as a technique to use before one writes a draft; however, many students find it useful to outline afterwards, as a means of detecting faulty organization or inadequate development. After talking with Todd, Suzanne might find it useful to construct an outline of her ideas before she begins to rewrite her paper, in that the outline would illuminate in bare bones form what has been created and what needs additional work. For example, if Suzanne had outlined her paper, the outline might have looked like this:

I. Exams cause a lot of pressure and make students question their fairness.

II. Exams cause pressure

  A. Students like to avoid pressure.

  B. Students have other engagements.

  C. Students become reluctant to study and may cheat.

III. Exams are unfair.

  A. Students sometimes bomb exams.

  B. Exams test trivial knowledge.

IV. Cramming doesn't lead to learning.

 V. Exams should be based on broad knowledge, not trivial details.

  The process of outlining highlights that Suzanne had not developed the concept of "unfairness" in the third paragraph, nor the section about how cramming interferes with learning. Outlining each paragraph might have enabled Suzanne to think more clearly about her ideas, to develop them more fully, and to refine her thesis. Of course, it is also possible that if she had written an outline *before* she began to write, it might have helped her focus her ideas more clearly. However, although outlining is often recommended, not all students find it useful, particularly when they attempt to outline before they know what they want to say. In the writing center, though, you might have students outline at least a part of their papers in order to help them detect faulty organization and poor thesis development.

  Tree diagramming is another way to create an outline. A tree diagram of Suzanne's essay would look like this:

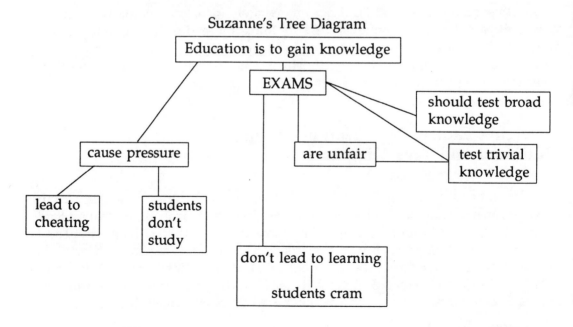

Suzanne's Tree Diagram

Whichever method you choose to use, keep in mind that the purpose of any form of outline constructed *after* a draft has been written is to focus student attention on its ideas and structure. The particular form of the outline itself is secondary to that goal.

## Other Methods of Detecting Faulty Organization

Students can also learn to detect faulty organization by focusing on how each paragraph relates to the overall thesis. You might ask students the question, "What is this paragraph about?" and "How does it relate to your thesis?" For example, if Suzanne had asked herself these questions in reference to paragraph #5, she might have discovered that the paragraph was more concerned with the problems of cramming than with the exam system. Other questions which are useful to ask are:

What is the function of this paragraph?

Does it develop the ideas in the previous paragraph?

Does it contradict the ideas in the previous paragraph?

Is it an example? Is it a definition?

Does it introduce a new topic?

## An Organizational Scheme Should Be Chosen Deliberately

Another way to help students develop a better sense of how to organize their papers is to ask them *why* they have chosen a particular organizational pattern. Often, they will discover that they haven't *chosen* the pattern at all—the paper reflects the order in which the student happened to have thought of ideas. Urge students, then, to reconsider the order of their ideas, and emphasize that an organizational scheme should be determined consciously. Point out that the order of ideas should be *graded* in some way. For example, if a student were writing about vacation possibilities in Bermuda, those possibilities might be presented in terms of how expensive they are (from inexpensive to expensive), how interesting they are (from ordinary to exotic), how time consuming they are (from short to long), and other ways as well. In Suzanne's paper, the argument that final exams don't facilitate learning is probably of greater importance than the argument that they cause pressure (after all, should *anything* that causes pressure be eliminated?) or the fact that they result in cramming. Since educational practices are usually justified in terms of their effect on learning, this argument might appropriately be presented first and given additional emphasis.

## Reorganization Can Create the Need For Additional Material

Work on organizational problems may reveal the need for additional subject matter, which may require more brainstorming, clustering or use of prewriting strategies. If this should happen when you work with students in the writing center, you should stress that this is not unusual, that the writing process is recursive, and that good writers often think of new ideas when they revise. In the example cited above, Suzanne discovered that she really had not addressed an educational reform in sufficient detail, that to propose the elimination of final exams was too simplistic, and that she needed to think about some alternatives. Of course, generating additional material means more work, and for this reason, students will sometimes resist doing it. As a tutor you can help students overcome resistance by encouraging them to aim for the best possible draft, even if it means more thinking and writing. To some extent, helping students become better writers means helping them aim for a higher standard in their work.

## Tightening Organization Through Transitions

You can help students develop a tight organizational structure and more coherent text by teaching them to use transitions in their writing. Transitions serve as signposts or cues to readers, pointing backwards and forwards within the text and serving to connect ideas. Below is a list of common transitions that may be useful for your students:

- Transitions that explain or introduce ideas: for example, for instance, thus, in particular
- Transitions that compare: similarly, in the same way
- Transitions that contrast: however, in contrast to, on the other hand, on the contrary
- Transitions that show cause and effect: thus, consequently, as a result, therefore

Transitions can also enhance sentence level coherence, a topic that is addressed at the end of this chapter.

# Working with Introductions and Conclusions

## Introductions

Students probably spend more time laboring over their introductions than they do on other parts of their papers; in fact, many students become so bogged down in the introduction that they never write the rest of the paper. One reason for this is that students are especially concerned about their introductions, since readers often use them subconsciously to formulate their opinion of the rest of the essay. Another reason is that students are often taught that the introduction must attract the reader's attention, and, therefore, they spend a lot of time trying to think of eye-catching strategies instead of presenting ideas in a straightforward manner. But I think that the most common reason that students have difficulties with introductions is that they attempt to write them before they have a clear sense of what they want to say and are thus struggling to introduce a topic before they have formulated a clear approach to it. My recommendation for such students is that they *not* begin with the introduction, and, instead, save it until the rest of the paper has been written. Once students have a better sense of what the paper is about, they often find that the introduction is not so difficult.

However, even when students know what they want to say, good introductions are sometimes difficult to write, and students may bring in introductions that are vague, do not clarify the thesis, fail to define necessary terms, or ramble off in directions beyond the scope of the paper. Of course, except for the necessity of containing a thesis statement (and even here, there may be exceptions) there is no one *right* way to write an introduction. As in all writing, the effectiveness of an introduction is determined by topic, purpose, and audience—however, if students need help in writing an introduction, they might find the following possibilities useful:

### Strategies for Writing an Introduction

1. Present a commonly held view and then contrast it with the writer's view.

   Commonly held belief

   *However* (or other word indicating contrast)

   The writer's view

2. Provide background and then present the purpose.

   Background

   Purpose Statement

3. Begin with several examples.

   Example

   Example

   Example

   Generalization

4. Begin with an illustrative anecdote.

   Anecdote

   Thesis statement derived from anecdote

5. Move from the general to the specific.

> General Statement
>
> Narrower Statement
>
> Specific Statement
>
> Thesis

These approaches are all pretty straightforward and do not include the zippy slogan or catchy descriptions that students have been taught are essential to a good introduction. In fact, so thoroughly have students been taught that their introductions must attract the reader's attention, that they sometimes write introductions that have nothing to do with the content of the paper! My feeling is that if students are able to incorporate a catchy introduction, they should do so, but if not, a straightforward one will be quite acceptable. Often, when students stop worrying about being witty or cute, they are able to write introductions more easily.

## Conclusions

Conclusions are not usually as problematic as introductions, but still can cause students some difficulty. Sometimes students will write conclusions which fail to conclude, leaving the reader without a sense that the essay is complete. Other times, the student will introduce an irrelevant or unnecessary detail, usually because he or she is having difficulty in thinking of what to say. If students are having difficulty with conclusions, you might suggest the following:

1. Refer to what was said in the introduction, either the context that was set, the historical background that was discussed, or questions that were raised.
2. Affirm why the topic is important.
3. Summarize the main points (but be careful of being redundant).

# Working with Sentence Level Problems

## Help Students Evaluate Their Sentences

Once students have worked on thesis development and organizational structure, they can start paying attention to the patterns of their sentences. Are their sentences varied? Do they connect smoothly together? Or do some sentences "sound" awkward, choppy, or difficult to understand?

Awareness of sentence level effectiveness and stylistic grace can be fostered through reading aloud—either the student reads aloud to you or you read their papers aloud to them. Reading aloud can help the student notice when the sentences are choppy and should be combined or when the prose is so wordy that one is breathless at the end of every sentence. As William Strong points out, many "professional writers . . . seem to spend considerable time hearing the way sentences fit together to make up the 'melody' of their writing." (xv).

Reading aloud focuses students' attention on sentence-level difficulties which actually appear in their papers, not on problems which happen to be included in an exercise book. Pay attention to the kinds of sentences students are actually writing. Then notice what kinds of sentences they are *not* writing as well. As Lindemann states:

> Instead of analyzing sentences in a textbook, students need to discover what kinds of sentences their own writing contains. Instead of drilling students on various sentence shapes, we need to show them how to create those shapes and how to handle the punctuation problems unfamiliar constructions create. Instead of discussing sentence patterns students already know how to write, we need to individualize instruction so that students are practicing sentence types they may be avoiding for fear of making mistakes in punctuation or subject-verb agreement. The goal of our teaching should be to enlarge the student's repertoire of sentence options and rhetorical choices (105).

Assign exercises, then, when the paper suggests to you that the student will benefit from them. Then, once you have assigned the work, go through a few examples with the student and show her how they apply to her writing. Don't simply isolate the student in a cubicle with an exercise book and then forget about her.

## Sentence Combining

If students are writing short, choppy sentences, they can benefit tremendously from work in sentence combining. Sentence combining derives from generative-transformational theory, which suggests that all writers transform sentences intuitively by adding to, deleting from, or rearranging kernel sentences. Sentence combining utilizes this principle.

Sentence combining exercises usually present lists of sentences, many of which are organized into clusters, each of which represents a part of one longer sentence. Students are asked to combine the clusters into one sentence and to experiment with different ways of combining them. For example, in William Strong's book, *Sentence Combining: A Composing Book*, the student is presented with the following two clustered sentences:

1.1  It was Friday night.
1.2  He was feeling good.

> 2.1 He had worked hard.
> 2.2 He had gotten a raise.

The student is asked to combine these four clusters into the following:

> It was Friday night, and he was feeling good.
>
> Because he had worked hard, he had gotten a raise.

Or else the student could combine all of them, as follows:

> It was Friday night, and he was feeling good, because he had worked hard and gotten a raise.

Strong advocates that students should learn to understand that "good" sentences are not necessarily "long" ones, but rather those which are appropriate to the context of the paragraph. Strong also advises student to "listen" to sentences by whispering them aloud and to experiment with new sentence patterns by writing them in a notebook.

In the writing center, you can work with students on sentence combining exercises (see the list of books you can use at the end of this chapter) and then go back to the student's own writing to see where the new knowledge can be applied. Sentence combining is not effective unless students begin to combine sentences they are actually using and to incorporate new sentence patterns into their own writing.

### Making Sentences More Readable

Although many students write short, choppy sentences, others write sentences which are wordy, inflated, unclear, tangled and too complex, making their papers very difficult to process. However, simply telling an awkward or overly wordy writer to "be clear and direct" is not particularly useful. Students must be *shown* how to write clearly, and then, perhaps, they will develop an intuitive feel for graceful, clearly written prose. A good way to show them is to make them aware of a few principles of *readability*.

## Teaching Readability in the Writing Center

Joseph Williams notes a very useful principle of readability which is quite easy to teach and which is very effective in helping students write clear, direct sentences. He suggests that the subject of each clause or sentence should be the *doer* or performer of each action and that the verb of each sentence should express the crucial action. For example, you might ask students which of the following two sentences is easier to understand after a rapid first reading:

1. The runner's fatigue prevented his qualification for the Olympic trials competition by a poor finish in the local meet.

2. The fatigued runner did not qualify for the Olympic trials because he finished poorly in the local meet.

Most students will agree that the second sentence is easier to process than the first one. Then ask students "why" they suppose this is so, a question which will focus their attention on the components of the two sentences. At first, students will probably venture that one sentence is longer than the other, but if they count the words in each, they will realize that both have approximately the same number of words. At this point, you can point out that the number of words in a sentence usually has nothing to do with clarity, rather that clarity is achieved by the way in which the sentence is constructed—that is, in the way each word, phrase, and clause expresses who is, or is not, doing what to whom.

You can then point out that the second sentence uses the subject of each clause to show *who acts*, who is the doer or performer of each action, and that it uses the verbs of each clause to express the action. The actor or doer, then, of a readable sentence is usually in the subject position. The action is usually in the verb.

| Subject | Verb |
|---------|------|
| runner | did not qualify |
| he | finished |

A few more examples will help clarify this:

In the following sentence, the subject is *not* the performer. The sentence is not written in a direct style:

A reapplication for her driver's license was necessary after her traffic ticket was given to her.

It can be corrected as follows:

She needed to reapply for her driver's license after she got a traffic ticket.

In the less readable sentence, the performer is *she*, but the subject of the sentence is *reapplication*. In the more readable sentence, *she* fills the subject position and the action, *reapply*, fills the position of the verb.

Here is another set of examples:

> *Subject not the performer:* The decision of individual grades will be made by the teacher after all the papers are completed by the students.
>
> *Corrected:* The teacher will decide individual grades after the students complete all their papers.

Once students understand this principle of readability, they should go back to their papers and rewrite some of their own sentences in a more direct style. They can also work on another principle of readability which is that vigorous sentences express action in a verb, rather than in a noun. For instance, in the following hard-to-process sentence, all of the major actions are expressed in nouns which derive from verbs (nominalizations):

> Upon completion of the orientation session, the one-month training of the salesmen with the sales managers will begin.

One can change this sentence into a more vigorous one as follows:

> When they complete the orientation session, the salesmen will train with the sales managers for one month.

Changing the noun *completion* to the verb *complete*, and the noun *training* to the action verb *train*, makes this sentence more readable. Two other principles of readability which students can learn easily are as follows:

> Avoid the negative.
>
> Eliminate unnecessary emphatics and empty expressions.

Thus, the sentence, "Not many students did not buy the yearbook," is more difficult to understand than "Many students bought a yearbook." State things positively whenever possible. In another example, the sentence, "For the most part, Majestic is a fast horse; the fact is, however, that for all intents and purposes any horse can beat him on a muddy track." is less readable than:

> Majestic is a fast horse; however, any horse can beat him on a muddy track."

The second sentence has been pruned of the empty "filler" expressions, "for the most part," "the fact is," and "for all intents and purposes."

To sum up, students can easily learn these four principles of readability:

1. The "doer" of the sentence should be in the subject position. The action of the sentence should be in the verb.
2. In general, it is best to express action in a verb.
3. Avoid the negative.
4. Prune sentences of empty expressions.

Other principles of readability are contained in the list at the end of the chapter.

## Teach Students to Make Connections

Transitions can strengthen the overall coherence of a paper and can also contribute to a smoother style. Transitions are achieved by a number of connecting devices: grammatical signals, such as conjunctions; punctuation signals, such as colons; or verbal cues, such as pronouns. For example, you might have the student read the paragraph below and notice the many connecting devices which have been used to tie the paragraph together:

1) Our family camping trip required a great deal of advance preparation. 2) Once we decided where we wanted to go, we had to arrange for campsite reservations, since during the summer, campgrounds fill up very quickly. 3) Then we had to assemble a great deal of equipment: a tent, a stove, sleeping bags, ground pads, a light, cooking utensils, and an ice chest. 4) Some of these we already had, but others we had to buy, rent, or borrow. 5) Finally, we had to plan our meals in advance, as we were not going to be near stores for most of the trip. 6) It was a lot of work. 7) But our camping trip was really successful because we had taken the time to prepare.

Some of the transitional devices you may note are as follows:

*Punctuation:* the use of the colon in sentence #3 cues the reader that a list will follow.

*Pronouns:* The use of "we" in sentences 2, 3, 4, and 5 and the use of "our" in sentence #6 refers back to "our" family.

*Summary nouns:* The collective noun, "equipment" refers to "tent, sleeping bags, and ground pads," etc.

*Rewording of the same idea:* "To prepare" in the last sentence refers back to "advance preparation."

*Parallel structure:* The grammatical parallel construction in sentence #4— "Some of these we had, but others we had to buy, rent, or borrow," emphasizes the parallel connection of the idea.

## Grammar and Punctuation

No question in composition studies has generated as much controversy as that concerning whether or not the teaching of formal grammar helps improve student writing. Whenever the "literacy crisis" is mentioned, someone is bound to suggest the teaching of grammar and numerous textbooks are published each year which include several sections of grammar based exercises. Yet several studies also suggest that "the teaching of formal grammar has a negligible, or, because it usually displaces some instruction and practice in composition, even a harmful effect on improvement in writing" (Braddock et al 37–38).

A useful discussion of the controversy concerning grammar may be found in Patrick Hartwell's article in *College English*, "Grammar, Grammars, and Teaching of Grammar" (1984). Hartwell maintains that "seventy-five years of experimental research has for all practical purposes told us nothing. The two sides are unable to agree on how to interpret such research" (106). Yet tutors in the writing center who wish to help students with sentence level errors often wish that grammar could provide the needed assistance; moreover, students are often referred to the writing center with specific instructions to "work on grammar." Students, themselves, are often under the impression that learning grammar will help them learn to write.

### Finding a Pattern of Error

Working with students on a one-to-one basis in the writing center can help you locate those areas in the student's own writing which may respond easily to limited instruction in grammar. Perhaps the student never learned that a comma usually follows introductory phrases or clauses as in the sentence.

"As I was going to St. Ives, I met a man with seven wives."

A simple explanation and a few examples can help students understand this concept. However, in looking for a pattern of error, it is important to distinguish between genuine errors and those due simply to carelessness. Having students read sentences aloud can help you determine this. Often when students read their writing aloud, they will correct a variety of spelling, grammar and punctuation errors, often without noticing that what they read departs from what they wrote.

If you do find an area where a limited grammatical explanation might help eliminate error, be careful that your explanations do not cause more confusion than enlightenment. Most students do not have a working knowledge of grammar; thus any grammatical terms you use must be accompanied by very specific examples of what you mean. For instance, suppose a student has written a sentence such as the following:

Singing in the shower, my foot slipped.

In helping the student understand this error, do not say "the problem here is that you have a 'dangling participle, since many students do not understand the word "participle." Instead, explain that the word "singing" must refer to a specific person in the sentence. The student will then be able to recognize that since no person is referred to in the sentence and since, obviously, it could not be the "foot" which was singing, that the sentence needs to be revised. A few examples of this sort and some practice revising sentences with similar difficulties will help students understand this sort of error.

## Limited Grammar Instruction

Students are frequently referred to the writing center because they write sentence fragments, run-on sentences, or have errors in subject-verb agreement; moreover, these errors are often those which most disturb readers. For helping students recognize these types of errors, it can be helpful for students to acquire a limited knowledge of such "grammatical" terms as "subject," "verb," "dependent and independent clause." At the end of this chapter is an exercise sheet derived from Muriel Harris and de Beaugrande which can aid students in working with sentences. Teaching students a few grammatical terms can also help you explain punctuation errors.

## Editing and Proofreading

Once the thesis is focused, the structure is set, the paragraphs are connected, and the sentences are varied, readable, and graceful, finally, it is time to edit the paper for error and proofread for spelling and typographical mistakes. This is the time for you to discern a pattern of error that the student can learn to correct. This is the time to instruct the student on recognition of a sentence fragment or a run-on, to test for the agreement of his subjects and verbs, to know where to place his commas. Numerous instructional materials exist on these relatively easy to teach skills, and computerized style and spelling checkers can also be extremely useful.

You can also help the student develop proofreading skills. Reading aloud to a friend or to oneself is an excellent way to detect careless error. Or you might recommend that students read their papers into a tape recorder, listen back to it without the paper in front of them, then listen again, marking errors and making corrections. Another suggestion is to have students cover all lines with an index card or book and go over each line, one at a time. Isolating lines can focus attention on surface detail and surface error, which may be lost in context when the paper is viewed as a whole. Or, another idea is to have students read their papers backwards. It's important, though, that students understand that they cannot rip the paper out of the typewriter or printer and then hand it in. Even the most experienced writer and the most careful typist has to proofread before submitting a paper.

You might have students work through the following questions when they edit their papers.

1. Are most of the sentences subject-verb-object sentences? Or are they wordy, passive constructions which use "there is" and "there are?"
2. Can any sentences be combined?
3. Do the sentences move easily from one to another?
4. Are there errors in punctuation? Spelling? Usage?
5. Have I proofread for careless error?

# Imitation

Although the goal of writing center instruction is to help students do their own work as much as possible, it is often helpful to actually **show** students a writing technique and have them imitate what you do. In the past, imitation was a preferred and respected teaching method; through imitation, it was thought that learners could expand previous ineffective methods into something more effective which ultimately became their own. Sometimes, then, it might be useful for a tutor to show a student how to develop examples, correct an awkward sentence, maybe rephrase something. Other suggestions might include showing students how to look for examples in a literary text or using the process of association to expand or redirect a thesis. Numerous writing techniques we have developed for ourselves can be acquired by students through the process of imitation.

## Teach the Student What Works for You

All of you were or are students; all of you have written papers; many of you will continue to write throughout your lives. Because you write, you have developed strategies which work for you, and these are the strategies you should recommend to your students in the writing center. Tell your students if you use scissors and paste to restructure your papers or about typing papers triple space so that you can revise easily. Maybe you work with a word processor or you xerox many copies of your early drafts so that you can easily manipulate the structure. Talk about what works for you, and your students may find your suggestions very helpful. A writing center conference should be a place where students learn the tools of the trade, techniques they can continue to use at other times. The strategies suggested in this chapter are only a beginning. You, as writing center teacher, will develop many more.

# Working with Sentences*

If you are working with a student who is having trouble with Sentence Fragments, Run-On-Sentences, or Subject Verb Agreement, this information can help the student identify these errors.

## 1. Finding the subject and the predicate.

All sentences have two parts, the naming part, called the **subject,** and the part which tells something about the subject, called the **predicate.**

Examine the following sentence:

The rabbit jumped across the field.
The actress flung her script out of the window.

**To find the predicate:** Make up a who/what question about the sentence. Eg. *What* jumped across the field? *Who* flung her script out of the window? The **predicate** is all the words in the who/what question which was in the original sentence.

predicate = jumped across the field.
predicate = flung her script out of the window.

The subject is the rest of the sentence.

subject = The rabbit
subject = The actress

**Practice** *Find the subject and the predicate in the following sentences by asking a who/what question:*

1. Mothers can usually figure out when a child is lying.
2. Dogs and cats are extremely popular pets in the United States.

*This exercise is derived from the work of Muriel Harris, *Teaching One-To-One: The Writing Conference* (Illinois: NCTE, 1986) and Robert de Beaugrande, "Forward to the Basics: Getting Down to Grammar," *College Composition and Communication* 35 (1984): 358–67.

3. Mary gulped down her sandwich and ran out of the room.
4. The room was full of furniture of all shapes and sizes.

## 2. Finding independent and dependent clauses

*Independent Clauses:*

An **independent clause** has a subject and a predicate and can stand alone as a complete sentence.

To find out whether a sentence is an independent clause, make up a yes/no question about the sentence, that is, a question which sensibly could be answered with yes or no. Eg.

> The rabbit jumped across the field.
> Did the rabbit jump across the field?
>
> The actress flung her script across the room.
> Did the actress fling her script across the room?

Only independent clauses can sensibly be rephrased as yes/no questions?

*Dependent Clauses and Fragments*

Only an independent clause can stand alone as a sentence. Some word groups are **"dependent clauses."** They have a subject and a predicate, but cannot stand alone because they need to be part of another sentence. Eg.

> Because she was insulted.

A word group such as this is a **dependent clause.** If it is used as if it were a sentence, it is called a **fragment.** Writing fragments instead of sentences can cause your writing to be graded down. To see whether or not a sentence is a fragment, make up a yes/no question. Eg.

Did because she was insulted? (This makes no sense) The word group "because she was insulted" is not a sentence, but a fragment. It would go well with the first sentence, "The actress flung her script across the room." Thus, "The actress flung her script across the room because she was insulted."

*Detecting Run-on Sentences or Comma Splices*

Run-on sentences are two independent clauses fused together. Eg.

> He hit the ball in the air the catcher made a grab for it.

A comma splice consists of two independent clauses linked by a comma. Eg.

He hit the ball in the air, the catcher made a grab for it.

To detect whether or not you have a run-on sentence or a comma splice, ask a yes/no question about the sentence. In a run-on sentence or comma splice you will get two questions instead of one. Eg.

Did he hit the ball? Did the catcher make a grab for it.

Run-on sentences and comma splices are other errors which can lower grades. Practice in these techniques can help students work with their sentences.

## Sentence Combining  *A Short List of Resources*

Christensen, Francis and Bonniejean Christensen. *A New Rhetoric.* New York: Harper and Row, 1976.

Daiker Donald, Andrew Kerek and Max Morenberg, eds. *Sentence Combining and the Teaching of Writing.* Conway, Arkansas: L and S Books, 1979.

————. *The Writer's Options: College Sentence Combining.* New York: Harper and Row, 1979.

O'Hare, Frank. *Sentence Combining: Improving Student Writing Without Formal Grammar Instruction.* NCTE, 1973.

————. *Sentencecraft.* Columbus Ohio: Girn and Company, 1974.

Strong, William. *Sentence Combining.* New York: Random House, 1973.

————. *Sentence Combining and Paragraph Building.* New York: Random House, 1981.

## Some Additional Ideas on Readability

Earlier in this section, I suggested four principles of readability which students can learn easily. However, numerous other factors have been cited as contributing to the "readability" of a text, among them:

1. Sentence length,
2. word length,
3. the number of prepositions in the text,
4. the number of different arguments in the text,
5. the inferences required to connect a text base,
6. the number of long term memory searches and reorganizations that are necessary to construct the text.

There are also about fifty readability "formulas"; however, what must be understood about these formulas is that they have preditive value only. If long words and sentences *caused* comprehension difficulty, then shortening them would remove the difficulty, a procedure which does not often work. For example, it is said that an abstract complex discussion is accomplished by many conjunctions, yet the conjunctions do not *cause* the difficulty— they are merely an index of it. Formulas are obviously limited. They cannot be discriminate between scrambled and well-ordered words or scrambled sentences or paragraphs.

However, although surface level factors do not by themselves determine the readability of a text, there are certain stylistic features we can help students become aware of so that they can make their writing more readable. Below are twelve techniques developed by Margaret McLaren which students can use to improve the "readability" of their papers:

1. Do not attempt to sound "important" when you write. Try to be natural. Most of us talk more naturally than we write. So if we can write accurately and concisely but at the same time recapture the relaxed informality—not of course the sentence structure—we use when speaking, we can communicate with our readers more effectively. For instance, we'd never say:

   > We regret to inform clients that the policy of this institute is to disallow applications for credit except in inordinately exceptional circumstances.

   We're much more likely to say instead:

   > Sorry, we don't allow credit except in very special circumstances.

   Why not write that too, perhaps changing the "don't" to "do not" if we need to follow the conventions of formal writing?

2. Use the natural subject-verb-object word order of English as directly as you can. Natural speech patterns make the subject of the sentence the agent or doer of the action.

   We tend to say:

   > Mr. Smith kept his appointment

   more readily than:

   > His appointment was kept by Mr. Smith.

   Passives do have a place when writers want to would hesitant or are reluctant to accept responsibility for an action. The sentence

   > His appointment was kept by Mr. Smith.

   may be necessary if we want to focus attention on the appointment rather than on Mr. Smith, but it lacks the punch of the active version. Try to state who is the *doer* (or agent) in the subject of the sentence. Try to state what is *being done* in the verb.

3. Use verbs rather than nouns.

   Instead of saying:

   > Our first requirement is the identification of the probable nature of the engine failure.

we'd do better to write:

We need to find out why the engine will not work.

4. Prefer the concrete to the abstract.

Instead of saying:

The new ownership has followed the policy of purchasing mini-computer type equipment.

we can simply say:

The new owners have bought a mini-computer.

5. Use simple words, if they mean the same as their longer equivalents, but be sure to use words appropriate to your readers. If you are writing for zoologists, "balaena australis" might be the best term; if you are writing for almost anyone else, "whale" most certainly would be better.

6. Prune "fluff words" wherever you can. When we're talking we use quite a number of words which carry little meaning but give us time to think. Early written drafts are likely to contain several empty words like "case" and "factor" and "situation" which simply weigh down the sentences. They may also contain wordy prepositional phrases like "subsequent to" and "in the vicinity of" which can well be cut.

7. Look closely at words commonly found in pairs, such as these:

| | |
|---|---|
| past memories | each individual |
| true facts | personal opinion |
| specified in detail | completely finish |

Often the idea can be more forcefully conveyed by one word.

8. Be sparing with impersonal constructions beginning with "it' or "there," and with verbs which do no more than link parts of sentences. In particular try to replace the word "is" which Richard Lanham (*Revising Prose*) calls the "weakest verb in the language."

The sentence:

There are sixteen people in the room who think. . . .

can become:

The sixteen people in the room think. . . .

9. Prefer the affirmative to the negative.

Not many candidates have not succeeded in this course.

is more dynamic worded this way:

Few candidates failed this course.

10. Spurn cliches. Imagery can spark up any kind of writing so long as it is fresh; wilted, it only makes writing look uncared for and takes up potentially useful space.

11. Vary your vocabulary, sentence structure and paragraph length wherever you can. If your sentences tend to be two or three lines long each, play around with them so that some are half a line long and others much longer. At key places use short sentences.

12. Achieve semantic closure as early as possible. The more a reader must keep in mind before achieving semantic closure, the more difficult the reading will be.

A sentence such as the following is difficult to process:

> Grandview school children, who were dismissed from school yesterday when a chemical explosion occurred in the surrounding area causing several thousand dollars worth of damage to plant and animal life, among them Mrs. Colingsworth's dog, Rover, not to mention her prize orchard, were allowed to return to school today.

## *Readability* *A Short List of Resources*

Kintsch, W. and Vipond, D. "Reading Comprehension and Readability in Educational Practice and Psychological Theory," in *Perspectives on Memory Research*, ed. Lars-Goran Nilsson. Hillsdale, New Jersey: Lawrence Erlbaum Associates, 1979.

Klare, G. R. "Assessing Readability." *Reading Research Quarterly* (1974/5), 10, 62–102.

Lanham, R. *Revising Prose*. New York: Charles Scribner's Sons, 1979.

McLaren, Margaret. "Another Approach to Readability," *Journal of Business Communication* 19, 2 (Spring 1982): 51–58.

Williams, Joseph. *Style: Ten Lessons in Clarity and Grace*. Glencoe, Illinois: Scott Foresman, 1981.

In diagnosing problems with a text and proposing revision strategies, though, be careful not to overwhelm the student with too many suggestions at one time. To quickly reel off what may need additional work can be confusing and intimidating for students, and some may then not attempt to do anything. So if you wish a student to learn some organizational strategies so that the next paper will be better organized, you should not then also focus on sentence level errors, such as sentence fragments or comma placement. You might aim for a policy of "one strategy per session." Or you might ask yourself the question, "What does the student now know how to do that he or she could not do before?" Asking this question will serve as a check against using the conference merely for "quick-fix" rewrites, from which the student might emerge with a revised draft, but without having acquired additional writing ability. The point to remember is that a writing conference should be used not only to point out to students where their work needs revision, but also to help students learn effective ways to revise. Don't simply discuss what ought to be done; suggest ways to do it, and, when possible, *show* student how to do it, so they can then do it themselves.

## Works Cited

Bartholmae, David. "The Study of Error." *College Composition and Communication 31* (1980): 253–269.

Braddock, Richard, Richard Lloyd Jones, and Lowell Schoer. *Research in Written Composition*. Urbana, Illinois: National Council of Teachers of English, 1963.

Hartwell, Patrick, "Grammar, Grammar, and the Teaching of Grammar." *College English* 47 (1985): 105–27.

Lindemann. *A Rhetoric for Writing Teachers*. New York: Oxford University Press. 1982.

Strong, William. *Sentence Combining:* A Composing Book. New York: Random House, 1973.

Williams, Joseph. Style: *Ten Lessons in Clarity and Grace*. Glencoe, Illinois: Scott Foresman, 1981.

# Chapter Seven

# Working With Non-native and Dialect Speakers

Gray suited Professor R. Q. Jones, of the Department of Business Communication, cannot read a student paper without reaching mechanically for a red pen. All of his academic life he has battled student error, with varying success, but in recent years, he has become particularly baffled and increasingly frustrated by the problem of ESL students who are enrolled in increasing numbers in his classes. "These students can hardly speak, let alone write the English language," he mutters to his sympathetic colleagues. "Their papers are full of all kinds of errors—verb tense mistakes, poor spelling, missing articles, mixed up sentences—how can I possibly give them a passing grade?" In desperation, he tells such students that they better get themselves to the writing center and have someone "fix up their grammar" before they hand in their work. Otherwise, he tells them, they might well fail the course.

Anxiety ridden Chon Thai, a student from Vietnam, is enrolled in Professor Jones' Business Communication course, a requirement for his Business major. In most of his other subjects, Chon is an honors student, and he can speak fluent, though heavily accented, English. However, he knows only too well that his written work contains numerous errors and that his concern with making a mistake severely limits his syntax and fluency. Chon worries about his writing a great deal, and the more he worries, the less able he is to write. So at the request of

Professor Jones, Chon comes to the writing center, hoping that someone there will be able to "fix up" his papers and make them more acceptable.

Due to open admissions policies at many universities and to a new wave of immigrants who speak English as a second language, students such as Chon are appearing in writing centers across the country. Painfully insecure, frequently the victims of what has been called the "karate school of Composition,"[1] such students urgently need the assistance of writing center teachers, not only to help them improve their writing, but also to enlighten instructors such as Professor Jones about the special problems of ESL students.

Ponder, then, the following three questions as you explore the issue of ESL students in the writing center:

1.  What should you, the writing center tutor, be doing to help students such as Chon with his work in Professor Jones' class?

2.  What is known about language acquisition and its development that can be useful to you as a writing center teacher?

3.  To what extent should you take responsibility for such students by helping to educate faculty members such as Professor Jones about dealing with ESL students?

Before attempting to answer these complex questions, I would like to establish that it is unlikely that a student such as Chon, however many years he lives in the United States and however much effort he puts into his writing, is *ever* going to write completely error free prose or, indeed, prose that doesn't "sound" awkward in at least a few places. With effort and assistance, Chon can certainly improve and can expect to write English appropriately and competently, but most people learning English in adulthood make at least a few mistakes when they write. In fact, many professional writers for whom English is a second language, use a native speaker to proofread their text for minor error or awkwardness.

Teachers such as Professor Jones, though, seem to believe that "errors" in ESL students' papers will disappear if they can only find the right remedy—stricter grading criteria, tougher grammar exercises and exams, more competent teachers, better textbooks. Ironically, helping ESL students to improve their writing skills has little to do with any of these "solutions."

Certainly, searching for the magic textbook is a fruitless endeavor. As Lil Brannon points out, the majority of ESL textbooks on the market today simply ignore all that is currently known about language acquisition and

> continue to advocate antiquated practices, operating under the premise that one learns a second language step by step, by analytically studying the component parts of English sentences. At worst we find the grammar traditionalists

---

1. Lil Brannon attributes this term to Donald Graves.

who see language acquisition as a matter of memorizing the basic 'rules' of English grammar and mechanics; at best we have the contrastive analysts who teach a second language in terms of the patterning of the first. Central to both perspectives is the assumption that students learn a language by learning how it is structured. (4)

However, there is no evidence to suggest that learning to compose and organize discourse is a matter of learning grammatical rules. Study after study suggests that what motivates students to acquire and use language is the "need to say something to someone who is genuinely interested in understanding them" (Brannon, 4) and that the mastery of grammatical structures evolves naturally with the students continued speaking, hearing, reading and writing of the language. Moreover, it is also generally acknowledged that students who are taught to concentrate on avoiding error rather than on generating meaning tend to write "a minimum of words in short simple sentences" (Vann 160) worrying not about how to make a sentence better but only about how to make it "right." Rather than risk making a mistake, such students never attempt new structures and sacrifice expression for correctness. Their writing becomes lifeless because it lacks an authorial voice.

# Second Language Acquisition and the Writing Center

Most linguists who study the acquisition of a second language now believe that adults have two "distinct and independent ways of developing competence in a second language. The first way is language *acquisition,* a process similar, if not identical to, the way children develop ability in their first language. Language acquisition is a subconscious process; language acquirers are not usually aware of the fact that they are acquiring language, but are only aware of the fact that they are using the language for communication. . . . The second way to develop competence in a second language is by language *learning*" (Krashen 10). Learning refers to conscious knowledge of a second language—knowing the rules, being aware of them, and being able to talk about them.

According to Krashen, acquisition and learning are used in very specific ways when adults develop competence in a second language. Krashen's "Monitor Hypothesis" postulates that normally "acquisition 'initiates' our utterances in a second language and is responsible for our fluency. Learning has only one function, and that is as a Monitor or editor. Learning comes into play only to make changes in the form of our utterance, after it has been 'produced' by the acquired system" (15).

Krashen further maintains that a variety of affective or attitudinal variables contribute to success in second language acquisition, in particular the motivation, self-confidence, and anxiety level of the learner. Generally, he says, learners with high motivation, high self-confidence, and low anxiety tend to do better in second language acquisition. Those with low motivation, low self-confidence, and high anxiety develop what is referred to as the "Affective Filter," (Krashen 15) which acts to prevent input from being used for language acquisition. Thus, students such as Chon, who feel threatened by the language learning situation, develop a high affective filter and find it more difficult to improve their language skills than those in a less intimidating environment.

## The Writing Center and the Affective Filter: What Should Students Work on in the Writing Center?

The writing center, with its emphasis on non-evaluative one-to-one teaching, is ideal for helping ESL students, in that it provides a special opportunity for students to utilize the whole range of language experience—speaking, reading, writing, and listening—and to have the tutor or teacher provide immediate, non-threatening feedback. In the writing center, the student has the advantage of trying things out and receiving an immediate response.

Ideally, ESL students who come to the writing center should first be encouraged to talk freely about their writing assignments, practicing fluency without fear of error, generating vocabulary and progressions of thought as well as developing a focus for their topics. Perhaps several of them who are working on the same or similar topics might come together to talk with a tutor in a "conversation corner" before they have attempted to write a first draft. Such conversations can serve to motivate students to acquire and use language in a real communicative situation; the tutor becomes the interested audience who genuinely is concerned about understanding what they have to say.

Or, if the student comes in to the writing center with a completed draft of a paper, the tutor can have the student read the paper aloud, enabling him or her to experience the text through two language channels simultaneously. Then, once again, the tutor can play the role of audience, feeding back to the student what the text seems to be saying, allowing the student to develop his or her own critical ear for prose and to evaluate the effect the text is producing.

Before working on surface error and grammar based disfluencies, then, ESL students should work on the same facets of the writing process as do composition students who are native speakers. They should be guided in preliminary prewriting tutorials toward generating a workable, focused topic, constructing a firm, organizational structure, and developing that structure to its conclusion before they think at all about correcting the surface. After all, there is little sense in having students edit a paper if that paper has very little to say and if what it says is disorganized and undeveloped.

Moreover, although Chon and students like him think that his major writing difficulties have to do with his inadequacy in the English language, and although Professor Jones is under the same impression, it is likely that Chon's most pressing writing problems are those of focus and organization. Like the preponderance of native composition students, many ESL students do not have a clear idea of what constitutes a well-developed text. They tend to write poorly focused, disorganized papers, undeveloped by concrete detail or logical argument. These difficulties are, of course, compounded by their anxieties about making a mistake and the limitation in their vocabulary and available sentence structures. So when the professor says, "Work on your grammar," these students tend to think that this is their major problematic area.

Examine, for example, the following paper, with the impressively complex title, "Advantages and Disadvantages of Television. How can We Eliminate the Disadvantages of Television? and you will see ESL related problems constitute the least of this student's writing difficulties:

---

## Student Essay

---

### Advantages and Disadvantages of Television—
### How Can We Eliminate the Disadvantage of Television?

Television made its first appearance just before outreach of the World War II, but it did not gain real importance until a few years after.

The television net-works followed the newscasting procedures that had been established for radio, with one important difference. Radio news had always been "live." In addition, the news being brought to the public through the radio, it's not as effective as through the television. One advantage over the radio is the television network crews in a few cities took pictures of events that had been planned in advance, and the film was flown to broadcasting station. This system did not provide coverage for unexpected events, however and newscasters make up for the limitations by reading a few news summaries at the end of the same shows. Television also present documentaries: detailed study of current issues, sometimes its shows including presidential speeches, interviews, Vietnam war which was telecast recently. Besides, these documentaries shown, there are also some good programs for children, such as "Little House on the Prairie," and "Sesame Street." These programs teach the children some basic knowledge.

Nowadays, there are other critics of the media. Some people believe that violence in the United States can be traced in part to the influence of the television entertainment programs that feature killing, fighting, and other violent action. And many studies of the influence of violence shown on the television show that these programs have some harmful effect on the attitudes and behavior of the young people. There are some teenagers after watching crime shows like "Starsky and Hutch," who may find that it is thrilling teasing the policemen. They could just rob a person for the kick of it. They may think it is a trip thing to do.

The invention of television give people a great attention. Television is being substituted for reading. This is extremely bad for those who really need reading because they may suffer due to less reading. In fact, some students may spend so much time watch television that their school work may be neglected. They may find that they do not have enough time to do their homeworks.

Many people complain about the low quality of television shows and the large amounts of advertising that appear on the screen. They do not believe commercial television should try to raise the standards or taste of television audiences. But the big audiences attract advertisers, and advertising is the key to success of commercial television. But this way, the businessman could make harm to children by introducing the interesting film that they could have the bigger numbers of audiences which is not suitable for children.

Basically, television is the entertainment medium. The advertiser buys commercials on the shows that attract the largest audiences. These include those that feature well-known stars and westerns, comedies, movies, spy shows.

Although television is primarily an entertainment medium, more people watch television and they receive their nation international news from television screen. Sometime they can see soldiers fight in a war on the other side of the world. They have seen and heard men on the moon. Television has changed their view of the world in which they live, as well as their lives at home.

In order to eliminate the disadvantages of television, the parents and the broadcasting stations have to play an important role. The broadcasting stations should make a point to screen those violent movies off the prime hours and if necessary then they can reduce them or minimum as possible. For example, in the morning, when most children have gone to school; educational and good movies should be shown at prime hours. Another way to eliminate the disadvantages of television is that parents should help their children to select the types of movies to watch. In that way, the children would not watch all those unrealistic shows.

❖

In the above student essay, the title alone indicates that the student has little idea of what constitutes a focused essay. The first part of the title, "Advantages and Disadvantages of Television," suggests a number of possible topics—advantages of owning or not owning a television, the advantages of certain programs over others, or, perhaps, as is partially the case, the advantages of television over radio. If I were working with this student, I would first ask him to explain his title to me. I would then ask him to define, if he could, the purpose of his paper and his conception of his audience—what he thinks his audience believes about the topic before reading the paper, what he wants his audience to believe about the topic after they have finished reading it. In other words, I would work with this student much as I would work with a native speaker.

Looking at the first paragraph, you can also see at a glance that the student knows little about the requirements of an opening paragraph. His first paragraph contains only one sentence and is, in fact, concerned with an entirely different topic than the one his paper is actually about. In the next paragraph, he begins with a brief discussion of the *history* of television. He then compares the advantages of television over radio, touching on a few minor limitations ("the system did not provide coverage for unexpected events."), then mentions a few programs suitable for children. In this paragraph, there are indeed some ESL errors—the improperly used "the" in sentence number four (*the* radio instead of just *radio*, the missing "the" before "broadcasting station" in the same sentence, the tense errors in "make," "present," and "including," and several spelling errors). Yet it makes little sense for the student to start correcting these errors until he has decided what his paper is really about.

As the student goes on in the essay, he touches on even more possible topics—the problem of television violence, the quality or lack of quality of certain programs, the stations' commitment to children's shows, the way in which television has changed the world. This student should be praised for the many ideas he has about television, but he also should be guided into focusing on one or two of them and developing them competently. The ESL problems of this student are relatively minor in comparison with those of focus and development.

In contrast, the paper below, "Enterance Examination to Music School" has many more surface errors—missing articles, tense errors, poor spelling; yet the paper contains a wealth of detail and a unity of structure, enabling the student to communicate feelings of futility and fright. As you read, note the black, shining grand piano in the center of the large auditorium and the cold looking thin lady, who parallels the coldness of the day and foreshadows the coldness of the corpse floating in the pool, the last image in the paper.

---------- **Student Essay** ----------

### *Enterance Examination to Music School*

That day was very cold. It was the typical day of January with lots of ice and snow. I was spending my second day at Gwan-Ack campus of Seoul University to take entrance examition of music school. In a waiting room with ither competitors, I was trembling, not becauseof cold weather but because of nervousness.

As the competitors were called by turns, my memories of all those years that I spent for this examition, flied to past. I had started to learn piano since six years old. Even though I quitted several times during my school years, still I kept playing till I went to high school. In 10th grade, I decided to become a music composer. From that day, every day with a continuance of hard train. I couldn't go to bed till one o'clock due to piano practice, to study music theory, to make music composition, to sing and to develop my ear to catch each single tone of piano key. Before I knew about music so much, I though music is just full of fun which makes people pleasent and comfortable. Sometimes I even cried due to the hardness of carring all those hard work. But now it was only a past and I am waiting for my turn.

Unlike my expectation, the room examition held was very big. Rather it was an auditorium. There was a black shining grand piano in the middle and I didn't see any judges. Only cold looking thin lady was sitting in front of the piano in perfect silence. I walked into the middle of the room and stood with insecurity near the lady. The lady passed me a piece of music which I was supposed to sing, automatically. Suddenly from somewhere upstairs behind the black curtain, one of the judges told me to start sing each note correct.

Could you imagine how I felt? Since I was so embarrassed even my legs and teeth started trembling. I regreted my careless practice forthat exam due to the lack of self-confidence. But it was too late. To pass the exam, I had to be one of the best fifteen out of thirty-five. Even I knew that I had to make exact sound for each tone and keep the rhythm constantly. I couldn't think of anything. I opened mouth wide to make sound but the room was still very quiet. I was so scared with the idea that I probably lost my voice because of nervousness. I racked my throat to have my voice back till the judges pressed me for sing. When I finished singing, I was so exhaused. I just walked the room silently without saying good-bye to judges.

It took about a couple of minutes when I realized where I was and what I did. I braced myself and tried to remember how I sang but only terrible feeling came up to me that I would be the worst one. I walked down the campus ploddingly. When I found myself in the middle of downtown, the street lights were already on. I though I should go home before too late, but I was afraid of waiting for the test result. I went to any theatre to spend time. It was "The Great Gatsby" which ended up with the death of hero.

Mother passed out and I was out of my mind when we knew that I did not passed the exam. Everyone took that as a joke, especially my friends and relatives who were busy with preparing surprise presents for me. Even though I guessed that

I was not a qualifier since I didn't get the phone call from the professor, it was a shock. Only the last scene of the movie which the corpse was floating over the pool kept acrossing my mind.

---

❖

---

This paper has structural and thematic unity, despite the presence of numerous ESL related errors. With this student, I would first work on smoothing out some of the gaps in the logic (If the student had prepared so rigorously, how is it that she regrets "careless practice," for example). I would then have the student read the paper aloud to see if some of the error is simply due to carelessness or whether the student is simply unaware of the correct usage or spelling ("the" typical day in January, for example, or the misspelling of "with"). Then I would work with the student on more careful editing, circling spelling errors, pointing out awkwardness in diction and sentence structure.

## Cultural Differences Regarding Discourse Structure:

Helping ESL students in the writing center also means being aware of the way in which culture affects the concept of discourse structure. Recent work in linguistics has shown that what is considered a preferred sequence of thought and paragraph structure differs from culture to culture. Kaplan points out that while English thought patterns are primarily linear, favoring little or no digression, Semitic and Oriental cultures prefer different modes of paragraph organization. For example, "maturity of style in English is often gauged by the degree of subordination. However, writing in Arabic favors a series of complex parallel structures (Harris, 88). Similarly, Karyn Thompson-Panos and Maria Thomas-Ruzic point out that the prose of Arabic students often is characterized by coordinating conjunctions appearing at the beginning of sentences "because of an Arab stylistic preference for emphasizing sequence of events and balance of thought, forms that favor coordination" (620). They also note the tendency of Arab writers to overstate a point and use what English speakers often perceive as excessive superlatives, an effect which derives from the Arabic linguistic tradition of over-asserted and exaggerated main points. Another characteristic of Arab written discourse, noted by Edward Hall, is the use of history as a basis for analysis of a variety of problems. Trained in this model, many Arab students may begin their compositions giving detailed historical background, details which may seem irrelevant or "off-topic" to native English writers.

Oriental students have other discourse traditions concerning writing which are also different from those of written English. Carolyn Matalene notes that

Chinese students are frequently trained to memorize phrases from classical sources and to use them without alteration in their writing. Thus, injunctions against using cliches in favor or original expressions seem strange indeed to these students; such advice contradicts all their previous conceptions about what constitutes "good" writing. Oriental paragraphs are also marked by greater indirection than "coherent" English paragraphs. "The Oriental student will circle around a subject, showing it from a variety of tangential views, but not looking at it directly" (Harris 99). They see the direct approach as rude, an offense to the reader. Thus, many of these students come to the writing center with instructions from their instructors to learn to come directly to the point and to support their positions with more concrete examples. Awareness of why students have these difficulties can help you devise strategies to help them.

Edward Hall also notes the distinction between "high-context and low-context cultures" (cited in Harris 91). A high context culture, characterized by extensive communication and close interconnection between family, friends, workers, etc., does not need extensive background information in written prose because the context is understood by all readers. Hall cites as example of high context cultures the French, Italian, Spanish, Middle Easterners, and Oriental peoples. In contrast, low context cultures, such as the Germans, Swiss, Americans, and northern Europeans, require the context to be explained within the text, and thus prefer detailed, explicit information. Thus different cultures vary according to the degree of responsibility expected from readers and writers, expectations which can substantially affect what is considered to be an acceptable text.

These differences in reader/writer responsibility affect all aspects of writing—not only paragraph development and contextual background, but also what is conceived of as textual unity. Harris notes that "English speaking readers will . . . expect transition statements to be provided by the writer so that they can piece together the threads of the writer's logic. In Japanese discourse such landmarks may be absent or attenuated because it is the reader's responsibility to determine relationships between any one part of an essay and the essay as a whole" (92).

Awareness of different cultural traditions regarding the style and structure of written prose can help you understand some of the difficulties foreign students have with writing English. You will have to help these students learn the rhetorical traditions and stylistic standards of English in written discourse, learning which may happen very slowly. But if you understand how differences in culture can significantly influence stylistic and rhetorical features of writing, you will be more likely to work with the variety of students you meet in the writing center.

What, then, should a writing center teacher or tutor do to help a student such as Chon with his work for his Business Communication class? My first recommendation is for the teacher to develop a comfortable working relationship with Chon, gaining his confidence, encouraging him to speak about his work, and scheduling a series of appointments with him to work through various drafts of his assigned papers. Although most students are uneasy writing papers, second language learners are especially anxious about their limited fluency, so it is particularly important for you to be supportive, to reinforce effort, to praise new areas of progress. Often, second language students have difficulty reading English as well as writing it, so it is a good idea to go over the assignments very carefully, highlighting key passages, ascertaining whether or not the student really understands what he or she is supposed to do.

Once you are sure that the student fully understands the assignment, you should work with him or her on the same areas you would work on with a native speaker—that is, narrowing and focusing the topic, strengthening the organizational format, developing each paragraph with relevant detail. At this point, only, should you begin to deal with ESL related problems.

Once Chon works up a final draft, though, it is the responsibility of the writing center teacher to make him aware that if he continues to write error-ridden papers, that he is likely to prejudice his readers against him, even those more benevolently disposed toward ESL writers than Professor Jones. Although it is unlikely that Chon will ever write completely error-free prose, it is certainly possible for him to write papers with fewer errors than he now does. What he must learn to distinguish are those ESL problems which respond easily to remediation, as opposed to those which disappear only after a long period of time.

## Strategies for Working with Non-Native Speakers in the Writing Center*

The following are some suggested strategies for approaching papers written by international students in the writing center; they should be used flexibly, as a guide, not as a set or rigid rules. The point to keep in mind is that non-native speakers need everything that native speakers need in the writing center plus

- opportunities to acquire language,
- knowledge of American rhetorical patterns,
- additional reassurance.

*(Based on research conducted by John Edlund at the University of Southern California)

## Beginning the Conference

Ask students where they are from, how long they have been in this country, and what languages they speak. This serves several functions:

- It breaks the ice;
- If you make this a habit, you can begin to recognize certain patterns in student essays which may help you in dealing with non-native speaker papers later (for instance, rhetorical patterns stemming from specific cultural differences).

Ask students what aspect of the paper, other than surface error, they, themselves, want to focus on in the conference. This approach encourages self-analysis and serves to direct attention away from grammatical correctness.

## Reading International Student Papers

Some papers written by non-native speakers are extremely difficult to understand. Therefore, to give yourself a head-start at overall comprehension, ask the student what the purpose of the paper is *before* you begin reading and then skim through the paper so that you get a global gist of it. To aid your understanding, apply your own world knowledge to the text and consciously strive to overlook errors. As John Edlund says, experienced international student instructors learn to *read through* language interference, similar to looking through a rain-streaked window.

Once you have a sense of the paper, read the opening paragraphs aloud to the student or have the student read them to you. This will focus attention on the main point or thesis of the paper.

## Working with Organizational Problems

If the paper has distinct organizational problems, begin discussion by emphasizing the paper's overall purpose, so that students will learn to look at sections of their paper as relating to an overall scheme. If the paper seems to leap from paragraph to paragraph without any seeming underlying development or connection, work with each paragraph at a time and ask the student the following questions:

- What is the purpose of this paragraph (an example? an elaboration? an opposing viewpoint? a definition? a qualification? a presentation of background information?)
- What does it do for the reader?

- How does it connect to your overall thesis?
- How does it connect to the paragraphs which precede and follow it?

## Sentence Level Problems

Since non-native students sometimes speak more competently than they write, it is sometimes useful to have students read part of the paper aloud and stop to rephrase sections orally that are unclear. If, as often happens, a student can verbalize something more clearly than what is in the original text, work with the verbal version, discussing differences among alternatives. A student who is very shy or self-conscious, though, will not be comfortable reading aloud and should not be required to do so.

In addressing grammatical correctness, about which many non-native students are extremely concerned, explain that grammar, while important, is best learned over time, and that the focusing and development of ideas is of equal, if not greater importance. If students insist on grammatical rules, point out that hundreds of "rules" govern any piece of writing, more than they could possibly use. Argue for the importance of tacit knowledge—a good example is that knowing the "rules" of tennis does not make someone a good tennis player. Most students, once this is explained, will understand and follow your lead, particularly if you project an air of confidence.

## Non-native Student/Tutor Interaction

Some students from other countries envision the tutoring situation as hierarchical and non-collaborative—they view the tutor as the source of knowledge and the student as the passive recipient. When students have such expectations, they do little to interact in the conference and simply nod at whatever you say or sit silently, despite your best efforts to engage them in conversation. Tutors often find this situation extremely awkward; moreover, they have no way of knowing if the student really understands or is simply being polite. A helpful way to deal with non-responsive students is to have them write something in response to a question. You might ask how he or she expects the paper to affect an audience. Or you can have the student list additional details, an opposing viewpoint, or a concept of audience. A conversation can thus be initiated when you have the student read what he or she has written. Another strategy for coping with this situation is to learn to tolerate silence. Often, if you wait long enough after you ask a question, the student may eventually come up with a response.

# ESL Problems Which Can Be Easily Remedied

Although many ESL students have spent countless hours going through grammar based exercises, they sometimes make a mistake simply because they do not know the proper form—a past tense of a particular verb, for instance. If you become aware that there is a specific structure that the student simply has not mastered, you should teach her the correct form, possibly refer her to an appropriate exercise, and then have her correct the error on her own paper. This final step is extremely important for any transference of learning to take place.

Many ESL students are unfamiliar with our system of capitalization and punctuation. Some seem unaware of the proper form used in referring to titles. Others have never made sufficient effort to learn proper spelling, unaware that poorly spelled prose irritates readers more than any other surface error. These areas can be learned relatively easily through the use of handbooks and exercises, and the student should be made aware of *checking* spelling carefully, either with the dictionary, a computerized spelling checker, or by having a native speaker quickly scan the paper for mistakes. (Of course, this emphasis on spelling should only occur after the paper is in otherwise final form.) Some native speakers may need instruction in using an English dictionary.

Often students for whom English is a foreign language typically have had more exposure to literature than to conversational or idiomatic English, and thus they have difficulty adjusting their writing to meet varying audience needs and expectations. Such students sometimes write with inappropriate formality. Or conversely, some students rely too heavily on oral language and thus transfer inappropriate aspects of oral language to the written mode. Run-on sentences or omitted endings (a common problem for language learners who have difficulty hearing or making certain sounds) are examples of this sort of transfer error. Students should thus be made aware that they have these difficulties so that they can learn the conventions and practices using them.

# Some ESL Problems Are Difficult to Eliminate

Some problems, though, particularly those involving verb tenses and articles, respond less easily to short term remediation. In these cases, after making sure that the student is familiar with whatever rules exist, it is often effective to have the student go through the paper paragraph by paragraph, checking for this sort of error. The student might also be encouraged to "buddy up" with a native speaker in the writing center, who can easily catch errors of this sort. The point to keep in mind about errors with articles and verb tenses is that because the rules are so complicated and because there are so many exceptions, it is unlikely that students will be able to master them through deliberate learning. Correctness in these areas is gained only through the gradual process of language acquisition.

The extent to which you, as writing center teacher, take responsibility for students such as Chon—that is, whether you decide to deal directly with professors such as Professor Jones—is a more difficult issue to decide. As Lil Brannon points out, the writing center often functions in a political context and writing center teachers often view their role as one of "adjunct" to the classroom, assuming that the referring teacher is the person ultimately responsible for the performance of the student. Brannon advocates that writing center teachers abandon the subordinate role and begin to view themselves as an integral component of writing instruction in all courses; this means grounding their teaching strategies in the best theories of composing known to the profession—engaging Chon in active dialogue about his work, providing supportive feedback in a non-threatening environment, encouraging him to read aloud and develop his ear for prose.

According to Brannon, writing center teachers ideally should view themselves as "philosophers of composition," whose mission is to convince the Professor Jones' of the university that emphasis on error in ESL writing can reap only negative results. And, Brannon, adds, if we are forced to choose between serving the student and adhering to the specifications of the instructor, it is "the student to whom we owe our support" (11).

Brannon's position is certainly a goal toward which to strive, yet it must also be recognized that it is unlikely that any new writing center teacher, teaching assistant, graduate student, or part time faculty member will have instant "success" in "converting" other faculty members to a more productive attitude toward ESL student writers. However, as a writing center teacher, you can keep your eyes open for opportunities to work with professors such as Professor Jones, becoming familiar with his assignments, developing a working relationship with his students. No communication can take place without some initial dialogue. And without communication, there is no possibility for change.

# Working With International Students in the Writing Center: An Overview

### 1. Work With Meaning, Not With Grammar

Although it is tempting to start with grammatical correction, you should focus on global issues—focus, audience, argument, organization—before dealing with grammar and syntax. Find out what the writing is about and what it is intended to accomplish before you make suggestions about grammatical changes. Make sure you know what the writer intends to *mean* before you alter the structure of any sentence.

2. **Use the Writing Center Conference to Help International Students Develop Facility with Language**

Many international student speak their native language at home and with their friends. Thus, they have only limited opportunity to speak and hear English. Even it you feel unable to help them with the various grammatical and syntactic problems you observe in their papers, your conversations with them about the meaning of their papers are a significant and important part of their English language input.

3. **Conscious Knowledge of Grammar is Not Necessary**

Because language acquisition is an unconscious process, you, yourself, if you are a native speaker of English, may not have conscious knowledge of grammatical terminology or rules. You know what the correct forms are but you cannot say why they are correct. Do not worry about this. Focus on talking about the meaning of the text.

4. **Common Grammatical Problems**

**Difficulties with the verb system.** Problems with verbs, both in form and tense, are common in papers written by international students. Sometimes, the problem is merely annoying, such as a consistently missing "s" on third person singular forms. In the most extreme cases, however, tense and person markers give such contradictory and impossible information that they must be disregarded in order to make any sense of the text at all.

**Other common problems.** Many international students have difficulties with articles, prepositions, count and non-count nouns, and problems with the structure of conditional sentences and relative clauses. Students are usually aware that they have these problems and are very anxious to have help with them. However, dealing with such problems in a decontextualized manner using exercises or drills is not very effective.

5. **Do Not Begin Correcting the Student's Paper Sentence by Sentence**

Students with massive verb problems usually have other syntactic problems as well. Thus, one could revise a sentence in a variety of ways, each variation producing a slightly or wholly different meaning and requiring different verb forms. Moreover, individual verb forms usually depend on global structures, higher than the sentence level. For example, if some of the verbs in a paragraph are present tense and some past tense, one needs to figure out what the whole paragraph is about and how it functions in the discourse before one can begin to correct it. It is possible to make a lot of corrections and then realize that a small change at the beginning of the paragraph could invalidate your changes.

6. **Keep the Student Involved and Talking. Do Not Assume Authority Over the Student's Text**

Ultimately, the goal of a Writing Center conference is to enable students to learn something that they can then apply to another writing task. If you completely take over the conference the student is not really learning anything, nor does the paper then represent the student's own work. Resist the temptation to take the paper over and "fix" it for the student.

# Some Typical Surface Level Errors in ESL Papers

Working with non-native speakers in the writing center usually involves focusing first on global areas of the text. However, it is also helpful to know about surface errors that occur frequently. Here is a list, then, that you might find useful in working with ESL papers. This handout is based on Mark S. LeTourneau's article "Typical ESL Errors and Tutory Strategies," *Writing Lab Newsletter* Vol. IX, 7 (March, 1985).

1. Nouns

   - Omission of the -s plural. (Oriental languages; the omission of the "s" after numbers [e.g. TWO UNIVERSITY]
   - Pluralizing non-count nouns or nouns used in their noncount sense (FLOURS, WINES)
   - Using the indefinite article a(n) with a noncount noun or a noun used in its noncount sense. (A FLOUR; A WINE IS GOOD TO DRINK [where the generic sense is meant])

2. Verbs

   - Omission of the 3rd person singular "s" (Spanish; [HE WALK])
   - Omission of the "ed" of the simple past tense (Spanish; YESTERDAY HE PLAY BALL)
   - Vowels in irregular verbs (SING, SANG, SUNG; BRING, BROUGHT; FEEL FELT)
   - Tense errors

3. Adverbs: omission of "ly"

4. Preposition errors. This is an extremely common error, attributed to the fact that the meanings prepositions express vary idiosyncratically across languages. For example, English says we speak IN a language, whereas Arabic says we speak BY a language. In some languages, there is no preposition meaning "at."

I prefer to live in home.
At the day of her arrival, we went to the airport.
The window was smashed with the boys.

5.  Articles. Omission of a definite article (Oriental languages. [I left my book on chair.] Insertion of articles where inappropriate. [THE EDUCATION IS A VERY IMPORTANT PART OF LIFE.])

6.  Word order errors.

    • Misplacing adverbs; (I WENT OFTEN HOME.)

    • Putting prepositions in the middle of the sentence. (He put in the corner the shovel.)

## Exercise

Read the following paper. In small groups, discuss how you would work with the writer of this paper in the Writing Center.

## ———————————— Writing Assignment ————————————

*Develop a thesis concerning a term or concept that is used both in your culture and in American society. Discuss how the use of that term in your own culture is similar to and is different from the way it is used in the United States. Be sure to include a definition of that term or concept and to include examples to aid in your explanation.*

## ———————————— Student Essay ————————————

### *Love in Hong Kong*

It is no matter what kind of country one comes from, what language does one speak or what kind of work or job. Every people need love to support their life. That is, love is very important, and no one can live without it. In Hong Kong, love means a feeling for someone of different sex. But it is a conservative word and different from United States of America. Here, the word is used all the time. One can say, "I love this dress" or "I love this dog," without thinking. But in my country, love means feeling of belonging to someone that one loves.

There are three kind of love—love of things or materialistic love, physical love which means attraction, and personal love, like friendship.

People say that "the love of money is the root of all evil" and it really does. Nowadays, materialistic love is so important that it is even more important than any other love. Especially people whom are in higher standard of society living would choose a materialistic partner forever. It is because they require a well-dressed manner and a classy look. Usually, an ordinary people does not like a materialistic partner because they know that they will not get anything in return. They are just pretending to fall in love with their partners, and this is like cheating a best friend. They want to cheat your money through the sense of love. From my opinion, I hate those lovers due to a proverb says "once bitten, twice shy." It is because they will hurt one's heart very badly.

If one gets a very attractive look, one will be definitely sure to be busy for the appointment of dating. The word attractive means that one should have a good-looking appearance and a good looking body profile. Also a nice smooth skin that is tan is important factor for girls and a strong muscular figure for the boys. Also some knowledge of beauty and body workout are essential. Because many people in the world are very selective. In the area of physical attraction love, love in high school or puppy love is an example of that area. In High School, appearance love is very important.

Well, on the other hand, almost everyone will agree with the proverb, " Don't judge a book by its cover." Which means that almost all of the people will consider that the personality love is the most important. The proverb gives us good advice, that it is better not to choose your partner from the appearance only, but from the inside of the heart. Personality love can last forever.

Another proverb says "love is blind," and for some people that is true. And for some people love is a trap. But a perfect couple should have the same theory as "love me, love my dog."

❖

## For Further Exploration

Anyone interested in working with non-native speakers will find it helpful to join TESOL (Teachers of English to Speakers of Other Languages). Membership in TESOL includes a subscription to the TESOL Quarterly, which is published four times a year. A membership application is printed in every issue of the Quarterly. For further information, contact

TESOL Central Office
Suite 300
1600 Cameron Street
Alexandria, Virginia 22314–2751

The following is a useful bibliographical essay with which to begin further exploration in this area:

Raimes, Ann. "Out of the Woods: Emerging Traditions in the Teaching of Writing." *TESOL Quarterly* 25 (Autumn 1991): 407–431.

Explanations of common ESL difficulties and some helpful exercises may be found in the following resources:

Huizenga, Jann, Courtenay Mead Snellings, and Gladys Berro Francis. *Basic Composition for ESL: an Expository Workbook.* Glenview, Illinois: Scott, Foresman, 1982.
Levine, Deena R. and Mara B. Adelman. *Beyond Language: Intercultural Communication for English as a Second Language.* Englewood Cliffs, New Jersey: Prentice-Hall, 1982.
Raimes, Ann. *Focus on Composition.* New York, Oxford University Press, 1978.
Ross, Janet, and Gladys Doty. *To Write English: A 'Step-By-Step Approach to ESL.* New York: Harper and Row, 1985.

## Working With Dialects

Some English speaking students who come to the writing center may speak a dialect of English, instead of Standard English, and these students often experience some of the same difficulties in writing as do non-native speakers. Alice Roy points out that both groups are, in effect, learning a second language when they attempt to write essays for school assignments, standard written English being sufficiently different from spoken English dialects, so that "acquiring a second dialect is a subset of acquiring a second language, differing at the outset in degree but not in kind" (44). Moreover, many dialect speakers, particularly those who speak Black English Vernacular (BEV), come to the university with a sense of inferiority about what they perceive as their linguistic deficiency. Since many of them do not realize that they speak a dialect, they are under the impression that they simply make many *errors* when they write; thus, many of them have had unsuccessful school experiences and are generally uncomfortable about writing. Yet within their own culture, their way of speaking has enabled them to communicate with complete effectiveness. In fact, were they to abandon their dialect and speak standard English, it is likely that they would experience some alienation from their own community.

Therefore, because many dialect speakers are, in a sense, learning a new language and suffer from similar insecurities as do second language learners, tutors should work with them in the writing center much as they would with non-native speakers, that is, they should address global concerns of a text before dealing with surface error, and provide many opportunities for discussion where students can hear and practice speaking standard English. With such students, it is also particularly important to create a comfortable, friendly atmosphere, so that students can explore their feelings about learning a new way of writing and will not be afraid of making a mistake. As with non-native speakers, explain that what has been labeled "errors" are simply the intrusion of one system of language upon another, that a second dialect is acquired slowly, and that they are unlikely to write standard English correctly right away, no matter how many exercises they may do. Provide a lot of encouragement, praise the quality of their ideas, and assure them that as they continue to write and receive feedback on their writing, their surface level "errors" will decrease.

In working with students who speak Black English Vernacular, tutors should also explain that their dialects are not inferior or sub-standard, but are simply *different*. Point out that Black English has a consistent system of rules, and that these rules would be just as difficult for a standard English speaker to learn as rules of standard English are for them. To help them understand why they should learn to write standard English, explain that dialect interference in a text can strongly affect the way that text is perceived by its readers and inhibit students' possibilities for academic and professional success; thus, it is in the student's best interest to learn to write standard English.

However, tutors should also be aware that many dialect speakers are concerned that acquiring standard English will cause them to become alienated from their own communities; therefore, tutors should assure such students that learning to write, and possibly to speak standard English, does not mean that they will have to give up their own language. Emphasize that this new learning will only increase their options.

Of course, there are some who argue that to encourage dialect speakers to learn standard English perpetuates feelings of insecurity, robs them of their "own voice," and represents a Big Brother-like domination of a minority culture by the middle class white majority. These views certainly have some validity; nevertheless, I tend to agree with a 1975 policy statement representing the editors of the *Journal of Basic Writing*, which maintains that although the journal generally agrees "with the ends sought by the opponents of teaching standard English: a more equitable social order and the psychological well-being of our students," it also believes that "these ends are better served when students enjoy the wider range of options opened to them by fluency in the standard dialect" (D'Eloia 9). This statement also maintains that "it is possible to teach the standard dialect without inevitably doing psychological damage to the student, provided it is taught in an environment in which language differences are explored and celebrated rather than stigmatized" (9). Surely, such an environment can be realized in the supportive atmosphere of the writing center.

## For Further Exploration

A useful set of exercises for working with speakers of Black Dialect may be found in Epes, Mary, Carolyn Kirkpatrick, and Michael Southwell. *The COMP-LAB Exercises: Self-Teaching Exercises for Basic Writing.* Englewood Cliffs, New Jersey: Prentice-Hall, 1980.

Some additional sources concerned with Black Dialect are as follows:

Carter, Candy, Ed. *Non-native and Nonstandard Dialect Students: Classroom Practices in Teaching English.* 1982–1983. Urbana, IL: NCTE, 1982.

Dillard, J. L. *Black English: Its History and Usage in the United States.* New York, 1972.

Labov, William. *The Study of Non-Standard English.* Champaign, Illinois: NCTE, 1970.

Shaugnessy, Mina P. *Errors and Expectations.* New York: Oxford University Press, 1977.

## *Assignment*

In *Hunger of Memory*, Richard Rodriguez, the son of Mexican immigrants, writes movingly of the conflict he experienced between becoming a highly successful student and participating in the life of his family. Read this book and discuss how Rodriguez's experience can be used to help students work with non-native and dialect speakers in the writing center.

## *Exercise*

What follows is a list of rules pertaining to Black Dialect. It is useful to understand these rules so that you will be able to work with texts written in this dialect. However, to get a sense of what these students must contend with, use these rules to write a paragraph using black dialect. I think that many of you will discover that trying to write in an unfamiliar dialect is not that easy.

### *Black English Consistencies*

Based on material by S. F. Braxton

("to be") Total elimination of "to be" in present tense

He a nice man. He *is* a nice man.

("to be") "Be" or "be's" used to indicate habitual condition

The soup be (be's) hot. The soup *is* (always) hot.

("to be" ) "Was" with plural nouns

They was at the park. They *were* at the park.

("to be") The future "be" without helper (will)

He be graduating soon.      She *will* be graduating soon.

("to be") "Been" without helpers "have," "had"

He been sick.      He *has* been sick.

"S" of the present tense eliminated

He play ball.      He *plays* ball.

"Ed" of the past tense eliminated

He play last night.      He *played* last night.

Elimination of possessive "s"

*Jane* bag is on the table.      *Jane's* bag is on the table.

Omission of plural "s"

I have three dog.      I have three *dogs*.

Pronoun Forms

Them kids      *Those* kids

Comparatives

This table is more better.      This table is better."

"Ain't" replacing "isn't," "aren't," "hasn't" and sometimes "didn't"

This ain't my house.      This *isn't* my house.
You ain't going with us.      You *aren't* going with us.

Multiple negatives

Nobody don't work here.      Nobody works here.
Don't nobody ever do nothing.      Nobody does anything.

"Going to" becomes "Gon" (and no helpers)

You gon' get sick.      You*'re going* to get sick.

Loss of final "l"

She's a foo'.      She's a foo*l*.

The dummy "It"

It was two people there.      *There were* two people there.

Elimination of final and middle "r"

He wants mo'.      He wants mo*re*.
He woke up do'ing the night.      He woke up *during* the night.

Dropping of final consonant

He passed the tes'.                    He passed the tes*t*.

Substitution of "D" or "F" for "TH"

Dey ran home.                          *They* ran home.
She hurt her mouf.                     She hurt her mou*th*.

# Works Cited

Brannon, Lil. "ESL Instruction in the Writing Center." *Conference on College Composition and Communication.* San Francisco, 1982.

D'Eloia, Sarah. "Teaching Standard Written English." *Journal of Basic Writing* 1 (Spring 1975): 5–14.

Dulay, H. and Byrt M. "Remarks on Creativity in Language Acquisition." *Viewpoints on English as a Second Language.* Ed. M. Burt, H. Dulay, and M. Finnochiaro. New York: Regents, 1977.

Hall, Edward T. *Beyond Culture.* Garden City, New York: Doubleday, Anchor Press, 1977.

Harris, Muriel. *Teaching One-to-One: The Writing Conference.* Urbana, Illinois: NCTE, 1986.

Kaplan, Robert. "Cultural Thought Patterns in Intercultural Education." *Language Learning* 16 (1966): 1–20.

———. "Cultural Thought Patterns Revisited." *Writing Across Languages: Analysis of L2 Text.* Ed Ulla Connor and Robert Kaplan. Reading, Mass.: Addison-Weley, 1987. 9–23.

Krashen, Stephen D. *Principles and Practices in Second Language Acquisition.* Oxford, New York: Pergamon Press, 1982.

Matalene, Carolyn. "Contrastive Rhetoric: An American Writing Teacher in China." *College English* 47 (1985): 789–808.

Roy, Alice. "Alliance for Literacy: Teaching Non-native Speakers and Speakers of Nonstandard English Together." *College Composition and Communication* 35 (1984):439–448.

Thomas-Panos, Karyn and Maria Thomas-Ruzic. "The Least You Should Know About Arabic: Implications For the ESL Writing Instructor." *TESOL Quarterly* 17 (1983): 609–623.

Vann, Roberta J. "Bridging the Gap Between Oral and Written Communication in EFL." in *Exploring Speaking-Writing Relationships: Connections and Contrasts.* Ed. Barry M. Kroll and Roberta J. Vann. Urbana, Illinois: NCTE, 1981. 154–168.

# Chapter Eight

# Working With Computers in the Writing Center

"I don't know how I ever managed without it."

"It's completely changed my life!"

"Everybody should have one."

Anyone reading these comments out of context might assume that they referred to some miraculous new drug, household cleanser, or cosmetic. The fact that these or equally laudatory remarks were made by writers about their computers' however, is a testament to the prominence of computers in the field of writing. Most writers, once they overcome some initial hesitation, find computers not only extremely helpful, but an absolute necessity, and many composition programs are now incorporating computers into their curriculum; frequently, these computers are located in or near the writing center. As a result, those who work in writing centers should understand what computers can and cannot do. This chapter suggests ideas and strategies for working with computers in the writing center and summarizes several types of programs that currently exist.

### Computers Cannot Replace Tutors

When computers began to be used in the teaching of composition, some teachers and tutors regarded them with suspicion verging on terror. Some had a generalized fear of machines of any sort; others were concerned that computer assisted instruction and computerized response to student writing would ultimately put teachers and tutors out of business. However, now that computers have been part of the academic scene for several years, it has become apparent that although word processing programs are extremely useful, and although database and spread sheet programs can count, sort, reorganize, and do all sorts of complicated mathematical computations, computers cannot deal adequately with an endeavor as complex as teaching students to write and think. Computers can ask students questions, but they cannot evaluate student response; computers can provide feedback about sentence structure and style in a text, but such feedback is helpful only when students know how to interpret and apply it. Word processors can provide useful assistance in invention, revision, and editing, but they cannot, by themselves, teach students how to perform these activities effectively, nor has anyone demonstrated that word processors enhance writing *ability*. Despite increased enthusiasm for the computer over the past several years, and despite considerable interest in "artificial intelligence," the computer still cannot respond satisfactorily to "meaning" in a text, and meaning is what writing and writing centers are really about.

If you are working in a writing center which uses computers, then, you should not be afraid of them and you need not worry that you are going to be replaced by a machine. Computers are wonderfully useful tools for writing (I would be lost without mine and wonder how I ever managed without it), but they cannot, by themselves, enable students to learn to write. However, as a tutor, you can utilize the computer as a means of facilitating that learning.

# Word Processing

### The Word Processor and the Writing Process

There are many computer assisted writing aids on the market today, and you may find some of them helpful. My own feeling, though, is that the most important computerized assistance in writing is provided by word processors, since they promote ease in invention and revision, and foster a collaborative spirit between writers and among writers and tutors (see Jennings (1987). When students write in a computer lab, they often assist one another, not only in the mechanics of using the machine but in the production of text as well. Somehow, when text is printed on a screen, it doesn't seem as "private" as it does when it is written by hand on a piece of paper, so students feel more comfortable about sharing their work with others and receiving feedback from fellow students. When a text is written on a word processor, students can work in groups to examine texts in progress, as the screen can be viewed by several students at a time (or even projected onto a wall screen by means of a data show).

Another advantage to using word processors is that since they make revision so easy, students can develop a more flexible, fluid model of text production. Because students can move text and work with it in different versions, they do not feel as *attached* to every word they have generated—they are more willing to *play* with their texts—to move sections around by cutting and pasting, develop weak sections with additional examples, rewrite introductions and conclusions, without the nuisance of having to retype the entire paper.

## Word Processing and Tutoring

If students bring in their papers on disk to the writing center, you, as the tutor, can work directly at the screen or work with students in conference; students can then revise their papers on the computer and then talk further with you about additional revision. Thus, word processors, while not specifically teaching students how to write, make it easy for students to write multiple drafts and to experiment with different models of the writing process, and it seems likely that a student who writes and revises frequently is going to develop a more effective writing process than one who does not. Of course, no study has as yet demonstrated definitively that word processing has a positive effect on student writing ability; however, one must also recognize that measuring the effect of *any* tool or teaching method on a process as complex as writing is quite difficult to accomplish. Therefore, since word processing facilitates both invention and revision, and since computers are likely to maintain their importance both in the academic world and in the workplace, students should be encouraged to word process their papers.

If you are fortunate enough to work in a writing center in which students have access to word processing, then, here are some general suggestions you might find useful:

1. Become familiar with the particular word processor in your writing center so that you will be able to answer students' questions about the mechanics of the program.

2. Encourage students to become familiar with the program. If students have to spend a great deal of time thinking about how the program works, they will be distracted from composing. The mechanics of the program should become automatic.

3. Whenever possible, the student's, not the tutor's, hands should be at the keyboard. Although sometimes you may wish to show students a particular technique, such as moving a block of text, students should be encouraged to work on the text themselves.

4. Encourage students to print drafts frequently and then mark them up by hand. Although some students have no difficulty reading text on screen, others find it difficult; moreover, reading a text screen by screen often prevents students from gaining a global sense of the text. A few studies suggest that when students work exclusively at the screen, they are likely to focus on sentence level revision rather on revising the thesis and structure.

## Word-processing and Invention

If a student comes to the writing center with insufficient ideas for a paper, you can suggest that he or she develop materials at the screen. One useful strategy is what is sometimes referred to as "rushwriting," which, as its name implies, means that the student sits at the screen and writes as quickly as possible without stopping. Rushwriting is, of course, another form of brainstorming or freewriting. However, if the student is a competent typist, working at the screen usually yields more material than working with a pencil and paper. This method can also be very useful when a student must respond to a text, an essay or a work of literature. The student can begin by writing their impressions of the text as quickly as possible, and they are often surprised by how much information they are able to generate, ideas they didn't know they had. Then they can print it out and elaborate on a few ideas that they especially liked, and before they know it, they have begun developing ideas for the paper.

Sometimes, students have not developed adequate typing skills, so that the mechanics of typing can interfere with their ability to think. If this is the case, then you, as the tutor, might sit at the screen and the student can dictate ideas to you. Once you have written down what the student has said, print out the text and use it to develop additional ideas. Of course, when you sit at the computer and do the actual typing, you may be concerned that you, rather than the student, are doing most of the work. However, if you resist inserting your own ideas, dictation at the screen can be a very effective method for helping students generate ideas, particularly for students who suffer from writing block.

Sheridan Blau at the University of California at Santa Barbara uses a technique that he calls "invisible writing," which means that students "rush write" or brainstorm with the monitor on the computer turned down so that they are unable to see what they are writing. Blau feels that this technique is especially useful for students who are so anxious about surface correctness that they are unable to write freely. Because invisible writing does not allow them to see their text, they cannot focus on editing at the time they are generating ideas. You might try using this technique for students in the writing center who suffer from writing block.

Because the computer can have a liberating effect on student idea generation, it is sometimes helpful to list a set of questions on screen for students to respond to. Some programs, such as "The Writer's Helper," consist of a variety of prompts which lead students to respond and thus generate ideas. Such prompts can be very useful for some students, although, of course, since no author or programmer can anticipate every possible question for every possible topic, the prompts tend to be fairly general. However, for many students, responding even to a set of general questions on the computer can lead to the discovery of ideas.

## Word Processing and Revision

The word processor is ideal for revision, as chunks of texts can be moved, additional material can be developed, and words and sentences can easily be manipulated. One model for incorporating the computer into your tutoring is that you and the student first discuss the draft in conference, decide what needs to be done, and then work with the student at the screen to begin the revision (or else students can revise the draft on their own and then return for additional discussion). If the paper requires a great deal of revision, construct a sequential plan, so that the student does not become overwhelmed and discouraged. Begin with one section of the paper at a time, perhaps the refinement of the thesis or a particular paragraph which needs development, and work on one task at a time. An important point to remember is that revision does not have to begin at the top of the paper and then continue down until the conclusion is reached. If a student is having difficulty with an introduction, then he or she might begin revising some other section. **Remember, though, to caution students to save their work and keep back-up copies on disk and in hard copy of everything they write.**

## Word Processing and Organization

Working at the screen with a word processor can be very useful for helping students work with a disorganized paragraph. You might have the student type a paragraph onto the screen and then work with it, rearranging and revising sentences to attain greater coherence within the paragraph, an activity that the computer enables students to do very easily. Sometimes it is also useful to have the student type all of the sentences in a paragraph in the form of a list and then examine how these sentences could be rearranged or connected through the use of transitions.

If you, yourself, work with a word processor, you may have discovered methods that work well for you. It is therefore useful to reflect on your own composing method and apply it when you tutor. Remember that using word processors to assist in the teaching of writing is still a relatively new idea—by experimentation and exploration, you may be able to create a whole new approach that no one has ever tried before.

## A Caution About Students and Word Processors

One potential problem with writing on a word processor is that even the roughest of drafts emerges from the printer looking neat, clean and ready for submission; therefore, even if the text is undeveloped, stylistically ineffectual, and filled with grammatical errors, students sometimes regard it as a completed draft. In working with word processed drafts in the writing center, then, remind students that clean print does not, in of itself, mean that the paper is finished. Have students read their drafts aloud and mark the hard copy to call attention to the necessity for additional work.

## Computer Assisted Instructional Packages

In addition to word processors, many composition programs have purchased computerized instructional packages that prompt and respond in preprogrammed dialogue to the writing of a student user, analyze a student text for certain kinds of surface errors, or provide opportunities for drill and practice. One such program, *The Writer's Helper*, addresses not only idea discovery, but also organization through outlining programs, and style analyzers, including number counts of words and sentence length, a report of "to-be" verbs, and feedback on passive constructions, undesirable word choices, grammatical error, and more. Many students find this program useful, and you may decide to work with it or some other program in the writing center.

However, in considering how to work with any program, you should first review the program thoroughly yourself, think about how you, yourself, might find it useful, and consider what philosophy or model of writing the particular program supports. Nancy Kaplan points out that "all of our practices are shot through with ideological statements" (13) and suggests that you ask yourself what statements a particular tool—a stylistic program or set of programs make about the nature of writing and the relationship between the writer, the text, and the reader. Similarly, Kaplan points out that "introducing computers into the writing curriculum . . . reintroduces old and familiar issues in new and sometimes unrecognizable forms" (28). Programs that focus on error correction and sentence level feedback, for example, reflect the notion that correctness and style are very important, and students who work with such programs may consequently concentrate disproportionately on surface, rather than global aspects of writing. Therefore, if students work with programs adhering to what you believe is an incomplete or incorrect model of the writing process, you, as the tutor, can compensate for its limitations by helping students understand what response from such programs actually means and pointing out its limitations. For example, some style analyzers provide readability levels of the student's text or counts up instances of "to be" verbs or instances of abstract nouns. When students receive this kind of feedback, they often don't know how to apply it to their own writing (any kind of feedback is useful only if it also implies an application). Thus, if students in the writing center receive feedback about "to be" verbs or excessive abstract nouns, you, as a tutor, can teach students strategies for reformulating passive sentences or making abstract nouns more concrete (See chapter 6). You can also help students understand that stylistic analysis is only one facet of the writing process, one which should be addressed only after the student has generated ideas and addressed the writing task on a more global level.

In working with packaged programs, the point to remember is that you, as the tutor, should help the student use the program and compensate for its limitations with your own ideas and comments. Do not assume that the program by itself can help a student learn to write. No computer program has the insight into text that a tutor has.

## Programs for the Discovery of Ideas

Several programs on the market contain sets of questions aimed at helping students discover ideas. For some students, these can be very useful, sometimes more useful than having a tutor ask the questions, because students feel a sense of privacy and ease when a computer, rather than a human being, is hearing their first attempts to deal with a topic. The computer will not laugh at their ideas or indicate that it thinks they are foolish or incompetent in any way. Moreover, the act of actually writing responses to questions often serves as a catalyst for generating additional ideas. As Ellen Nold pointed out more than fifteen years ago, "the computer provides a patient and non-threatening, fluid and provocative backboard against which to bounce ideas (271). Sometimes students find them more useful than talking to a tutor.

One early application of invention strategies to the computer was initiated by Hugh Burns, who applied classical invention heuristics to the screen as a means of prompting student information. After the student inputs an idea, the program provides encouragement with positive response, such as "Good, John. Anything else?" Other discovery programs are geared more specifically toward typical freshman assignments, such as narration, description, or persuasion.

These programs can be useful, although they have been criticized as being overly generalized and oversimplified. Students will sometimes enter wisecracks instead of exploratory discourse, and since the computer has no way of evaluating the quality of the response, it has no way of responding appropriately. It will still say "Good, John. Anything else?" no matter what the student writes. Hashimoto criticizes such programs as "optimistic" and "oversimplified" (73) in that they cannot accommodate individual learning and writing styles. Sirc similarly observes that structured discovery programs can exclude the serendipity that less structured, more associative methods of prewriting can facilitate.

As a general principle, then, computers can serve as a valuable tool in the writing center if they foster enlightenment about the writing process and facilitate the generation and revision of text. However, despite general enthusiasm about computers and composition, despite numerous articles, conference presentations, and new software development, we are only at the beginning of discovering how computers can be applied to the teaching of writing. As a tutor in the writing center, you are in an excellent position to participate in that discovery.

## Two Specialized Programs to Note

THE RESEARCHER'S ELECTRONIC NOTEBOOK—a hypertext program for helping students write research papers. See

Clark, Irene Lurkis. "The Writing Center and the Research Paper: Computers and Collaboration." in Ray Wallace, ed. The Writing Center: New Directions. New York: Garland, 1991. 205–216.

SEEN—provides an open-ended tutorial for examination of texts. Feedback is provided by peers who share ideas on a bulletin board included as part of the program. See

Schwartz, Helen. "Seen: A Tutorial and User Network for Hypothesis Testing." in William Wresch, ed. *The Computer in Composition Instruction: A Writer's Tool.* Urbana: NCTE, 1984. 47–52.

A useful publication to keep current with new ideas in computers and composition is the journal of that name, *Computers and Composition.* To subscribe, contact

Dr. Cynthia Selfe
*Computers in Composition*
c/o Accounting Office
Michigan Technological University
Houghton, MI 49931

# For Further Exploration

Burns, Hugh. "Recollections of First-Generation Computer-Assisted Prewriting. In *The Computer in Composition Instruction: A Writer's Tool*. ed. W. Wresch. Urbana, Ill: NCTE, 1984.

Collier, R. M. "The Word Processor and Revision Strategies." *College Composition and Communication 34* (1983): 149–155.

Haas, C. "How the Writing Medium Shapes the Writing Process: Effects of Word Processing on Planning." *Research in the Teaching of English 23* (1989): 181–207.

Haas, C. "Seeing It On the Screen Isn't Really Seeing It: Computer Writers' Reading Problems." in G.E. Hawisher and C. L. Selfe (Eds) *Critical Perspectives in Computers and Composition Instruction* (pp. 16–29): New York: Teachers College Press, 1989.

Haas, C. and L. R. Hayes. "What Did I Just Say? Reading Problems in Writing with the Machine." *Research in the Teaching of English 10* (1986): 22–35.

Hashimoto, I. "Structured Heuristic Procedures: Their Limitations." *College Composition and Communication 36* (1985): 73–81.

Holdstein, Deborah H. and Cynthia L. Selfe. *Computers and Writing: Theory, Research, Practice*. New York: MLA, 1990.

Jennings, Edward M. "Paperless Writing: Boundary Conditions and Their Implications." In L. Gerrard (Ed) *Writing At Century's End: Essays on Computer Assisted Composition*. New York: Random House, 1987. 11–20.

Kaplan, Nancy. "Ideology, Technology, and the Future of Writing Instruction." In Gail Hawisher and Cynthia L. Selfe (Eds.) *Evolving Perspectives on Computers and Composition Studies: Questions For the 1990's*. Urbana: NCTE, 1991. 11–43.

Nold, Ellen. "Fear and Trembling: The Humanist Approaches the Computer. *College Composition and Communication 26* (1975): 269–273.

Parson, Gail. *The Writing Process and the Microcomputer*. Urbana: NCTE, 1985.

Rodrigues, R. J. and Rodgriguez, D. W. "Computer Based Invention: Its Place and Potential." *College Composition and Communication 35* (1984): 78–87.

Rodriquez, D. W. "Computers and Basic Writers." *College Composition and Communication*, 36 (October 1985): 336–339.

Selfe, Cynthia and Gail Hawisher, eds. *Critical Perspectives on Computers and Composition*. New York: Teachers College Press, 1989.

Sirc, Geoffrey. "Response in the Electronic Medium." In Chris M. Anson (Ed.) *Writing and Response: Theory, Practice and Research*. Urbana: NCTE, 1989. 187–205.

Spitzer, Michael. "Incorporating Prewriting Software into the Writing Program." in C. L. Selfe, D. W. Rodriguez, and W. R. Oates (Eds) *Computers in English and the Language Arts*. NCTE: Urbana, Ill., 1989. 205–212.

Standiford, Sally N., Kathleen Jaycox, and Anne Auten. *Computers in the English Classroom*. Urbana: NCTE, 1983.

Wresch, William, ed. *The Computer in Composition Instruction: A Writer's Tool*. Urbana: NCTE, 1984.

# Chapter Nine

# Special Assignments:
# The Research Paper and the Literary Essay

This chapter is concerned with a few of the special assignments that students often bring to the writing center. In particular, I will address the "research" paper, including difficulties students have in working with sources, and papers concerned with literature, including book review assignments. Of course, in one chapter, I cannot discuss these genres thoroughly; however, I can give you some ideas that may help you work with students more effectively and I will also include a list of references so that you can pursue these topics on your own.

## Undergraduate "Research" Papers: Some Common Problems

When students are assigned what has traditionally been called the "research" paper, they often bring in some depressingly unsatisfactory writing. Because they are confused about what is expected of them, students simply find a lot of quotations and paste them together, rather than using them to support a well-developed thesis. Thus, their papers are often excessively long and pointless, overly generalized, disorganized, unfocused and occasionally plagiarized. The main reason these papers are so poor is that many students don't realize that research oriented essays, like other essays, should usually have a main point, and thus they use sources, not to support that main point, but simply to show their instructors how much information they have found. Consequently, their papers are a collage of quotations that often don't connect coherently to a central idea.

Writing center tutors who are aware of this problem, then, should begin to work with students on research papers in the same way they would work with them on other types of assignments—on developing and shaping a thesis. As in working with other unfocused papers, I suggest that you begin by asking students what their papers are about, have them tell you what their thesis is, and summarize their main supporting points. Then, when you read the paper, you will be able to compare what is written to what the student has stated as the main point. You can also have students write down a thesis statement while you read the paper or indicate how the paper is intended to influence an audience. These activities will emphasize that the "research" paper is supposed to develop a thesis, and once students understand the purpose of their research paper assignments, they often have less difficulty with them.

However, even when students understand the purpose of research paper assignments, they may encounter additional problems—typically, the ability to plan time, take and synthesize notes, and incorporate sources smoothly into their papers. You may find some of the suggestions in this chapter useful for helping students with these difficulties.

## The Research Paper Time Management Form*

If students come to the writing center as soon as they receive their research paper assignment, you can help them plan their time, since papers involving research usually require some library work, outside reading, and notetaking, as well as time for drafting and revising. On the following page is a form you may wish to use with students when they begin to work on their research papers.

## Taking and Synthesizing Notes**

You can also work with students on their research papers by helping them develop note taking and note synthesizing strategies. Many students are unaware of *why* one takes notes, and they, therefore, take notes on everything they read. Then, when they start actually writing the paper, they have a set of copious notes but don't know which ones they ought to include and have difficulty organizing

---

*This form is adapted from: Clark, Irene L. *Taking a Stand: A Guide to the Researched Paper With Readings.* New York: Harper Collins, 1992.

**Both the Source Notesheet and the Note Synthesis Sheet may also be found in: Clark, Irene Lurkis. *Taking a Stand: A Guide to the Researched Paper with Readings.* New York: Harper Collins, 1992.

## RESEARCH PAPER TIME MANAGEMENT FORM

| Research Activity | When? | Where? |
|---|---|---|
| Reading assignment | | |
| Writing Exploratory draft | | |
| Reading sources | | |
| Brainstorming | | |
| Developing preliminary topic | | |
| Creating an outline | | |
| Writing First draft | | |
| Getting Feedback on first draft | | |
| Writing second draft | | |
| Revising second draft | | |
| Editing second draft | | |
| Checking documentation | | |
| Printing and copying | | |

them. The two sheets below are useful for helping students record and synthesize their notes.

The **Source Notesheet** is used to record notes about a single source and contains information only from that source. The first piece of information the student records is the author's last name, so that these sheets can be alphabetized to create the bibliography. There is also a place on this sheet for a brief summary of the source, to help the student remember what the overall purpose of the source was.

In working with this sheet, point out to students the section marked "Idea About Note." That section can be used to record ideas that student might have for actually using the note in the paper—for example, the student might write, "This would make a good argument against the general viewpoint" or "This is a good example of _____." The Source Notesheet provides a place to help students jot down ideas, so that they don't lose interesting thoughts as they occur.

# SOURCE NOTE SHEET

Author(s)
Title
Journal
Publisher
Date, Place
Pages

| Page # | Note | Idea About Note |
|--------|------|-----------------|
|        |      |                 |

The **Note Synthesis Sheet** helps students organize notes around a particular aspect of a topic and allows them to combine information from several sources. One advantage of using the Note Synthesis Sheet is that the column marked "Reason for Using" focuses student attention on *why* they may choose to incorporate a particular quotation or paraphrase. For example, does the quotation or paraphrase provide an example? Does it support the thesis? Does it establish authority? Does it contradict someone else's point of view? These are important questions for students to ask themselves, so that they don't fill their papers with too many quotations simply to display how many sources they have found. The Note Synthesis Sheet thus emphasizes the importance of using the opinions of others for a particular purpose. However, if a student brings in a draft which consists simply of a string of quotations, a useful strategy is to have them highlight all of the quotations with a marker. This will illustrate in living color what percentage of the paper is quotation and how little of their own writing there actually is. Point out that papers without a personal voice are usually lifeless and uninteresting to read.

## Common Student Problems in Using Quotations

### The "Crouton" Effect

One common problem exhibited in research papers brought to the writing center is that of incorporating quotations and paraphrases smoothly into the text. Often students seem to just sprinkle them in, like croutons in a salad, so that they never seem to blend in. Here is an example:

---

### Student Essay

---

Although many people are under the impression that smoking marijuana has had no effect on them, some recent research studies indicate that it has an effect on the heart, lungs, and brain. "All the subjects had significant lung function impairment in several areas. These impairments were similar to those found by other researchers studying people who had smoked tobacco moderately to heavily for many years" (Mann 115).

---

---

In this example, the quotation is not framed by a reference to where the study was done or how the study illustrates the writer's point. In working with students on incorporating quotations, you can suggest that they **refer to the source in some way,** usually by mentioning the author or title, indicating the

# NOTE SYNTHESIS SHEET

Subject of Paper

Sub-Topic

| Source | Page # | Note | Reason For Using |
|--------|--------|------|------------------|
|        |        |      |                  |

source's attitude or position by using a verb, or showing the source's relevance to the point being made. Some useful verbs to suggest are as follows:

| indicates | exemplifies |
|-----------|-------------|
| observes | argues |
| explains | suggests |
| describes | advocates |

Here is a possible revision of the above paragraph:

Although many people are under the impression that smoking marijuana has had no effect on them, some recent research studies indicate that it has an effect on the heart, lungs, and brain. A study of marijuana smokers conducted at UCLA suggests such an effect. In fact, as Peggy Mann points out, "All the subjects had significant lung function impairment in several areas. These impairments were similar to those found by other researchers studying people who had smoked tobacco moderately to heavily for many years" (Mann 115).

Another problem students often have with using quotations is that of framing them gracefully. They will write a sentence such as this:

In Peggy Mann's discussion of a marijuana research study, she says . . .

Students should be taught that it is not necessary to repeat the word "she" in this construction, that there are other ways of saying "says," and that framing or contextual references can appear in the middle or end of a sentence, not just at the beginning.

Thus, the above sentence could be rephrased in many possible ways, such as:

In her discussion of a marijuana research study, Peggy Mann says (indicates, suggests, maintains, states, points out, reveals, shows, etc.)
    or

Research on marijuana smoking indicates its effect on the lungs, heart, and brain, an effect, which, as Peggy Mann points out, is "similar to those found by other researchers studying people who had smoked tobacco moderately to heavily for many years" (115).

Difficulties in incorporating quotations can often be detected if either you or the student reads the text aloud.

*Exercise*

A student has come into the writing center with a draft of his research paper, reprinted below. Read the paper and then, in small groups, use the discussion questions to examine how you would work with this student.

——————————————— **Writing Assignment** ———————————————

*Select a section from Studs Terkel's Working. Write a paper examining the extent to which this section pertains to working conditions today.*

——————————————— **Student Essay** ———————————————

### *The Alienation of the American Laborer: The Case of Mike Lefevre*

Mike Lefevre is a laborer. He works in a steel mill from seven o'clock in the morning to three o'clock in the afternoon. He has a wife and two children. On occasion, his wife will work, but he is the primary moneymaker. He doesn't care for his boss and has no respect for any kind of management. He insults and cuts down higher education, while at the same time wants his own children to go to college so they won't end up like him. On the weekends, he goes from tavern to tavern to get drunk and forget about his job. He is part of the work force that keeps America going. He is part of an assembly-line process that has built this country. He is a faceless, nameless part of a larger machine. **He is the American worker.**

Mike Lefevre is part of a work force that has become alienated from their work. Their job has become "a duty and an obsession." (Fromm, Work in an Alienated Society, p. 530). The meaning behind their work has disappeared. When once a worker "could point to a house he built, how many logs he stacked. He built it and he was proud of it." (Terkel, Mike Lefevre, p. 520–521). Now it is "something unnatural, a disagreeable, meaningless, and stultifying condition of getting the pay check, devoid of dignity as well as of importance" (Fromm, Work in an Alienated Society, p. 531).

The case of Mike Lefevre began to form in the eighteenth century. The belief that "virtue pays . . . but what it pays cannot be measured simply in money" (Lasch, The Original Meaning of the Work Ethic, p. 537) began to falter as the practice of self-preservation replace self-improvement. "They hope not so much to prosper as to survive." (Lasch, The Original Meaning of the Work Ethic, p. 535). Christopher Lasch summed up this change in this essay titled *The Original Meaning of the Work Ethic* by saying "the self-made man took pride in his judgment of character and probity; today he anxiously scans the faces of his fellows not so as to evaluate their credit, but in order to guage their susceptibility to his own blandishments." (p. 535).

"In the nineteenth century, the ideal of self-improvement degenerated into a cult of compulsive industry." (Lasch, The Original Meaning of the Work Ethic, p. 538). According to Lasch, the people of the nineteenth century tried to put a monetary amount of all values. There was a price tag on everything, no matter how big or how small. Lasch states that "the eighteenth century made a virtue of temperance, but did not condemn moderate indulgence in the service of sociability. . . . The nineteenth century condemned sociability on the grounds that it night interfere with business." (Lasch, The Original Meaning of the Work Ethic, p. 538). As the century ended and the twentieth century began, this belief was passed on. Because of this belief, the alienation of the worker from his job occurred.

At work, the management is concerned with productivity, not how their workers feel. This occurs "when policy making, the search for power, and the pursuit of wealth have no other objects than to excite admiration or envy." (Lasch, the Original Meaning of the Work Ethic, p. 542). Lefevre shows contempt and disrespect to his superiors. He won't say hello or good morning. On at least two occasions, they have physically fought, causing Lefevre to be demoted or "broke down to a lower grade." (Terkel, Mike Lefevre, p. 522). This tension, this conflict between management and laborer can be traced back to Lasch's eighteenth and nineteenth century.

Lefevre's alienation from his work lead to daydreams and fantasies about self-improvement. Lefevre is numb and unfeeling during his eight-hour workday that he must pass the time somehow. In one fantasy, he runs "a combination bookstore and tavern. . . . I would like to have place where college kids came and a steelworker could sit down and talk. Where a workingman could not be ashamed of Walt Whitman and where a college professor could not be ashamed that he painted his house over the weekend." (Terkel, Mike Lefevre, p. 527). Self-improvement is a part of Lefevre's life. If he could, he would save money to send his kids to college. He would save money to get a better place to live. But the self-preservation and the week-by-week survival prevails. This kind of wishful thinking tells the public that something is not right in the American workplace.

The alienation in the workplace leads to the laborer being an anonymous piece of machinery. The laborer loses his identity. "Way back, you spoke of the guys who built the pyramids, not the pharaohs, but the unknowns. You put yourself in their category? . . . Yes. I want my signature on 'em, too. Sometimes, out of pure meanness, when I make something, I put a little dent in it. I like to do something unique." (Terkel, Mike Lefevre, p. 528). It is because of the assembly-line process under which American industry is run that the laborer must resort to such measures to "make his mark" so he does not completely lose his identity.

Another aspect of American industry that further alienates the laborer is the threat of automation. With technology improving greatly each year, computers are becoming an essential part of our lives. How does Lefevre feel about automation? "Automation? Depends on how it's applied. It frightens me in it puts me on the street. It doesn't frighten me if it shortens my work week." (Terkel, Mike Lefevre, p. 523). Lefevre also feels that "machines can either liberate man or enslave 'im, because they're pretty neutral." (Terkel, Mike Lefevre, p. 523).

Alienation in the workplace began as early as the nineteenth century. It has progressively gotten worse as time goes on. Self-preservation plays a vital role in the life of the American laborer. He/she must work, suffer anonymity, and money-hungry management to keep food on the table for the family. The case of Mike Lefevre is stereotypical. His desire for something better, his wish for recognition, and his wariness of automation tell the story of the American laborer. The past has created the present. The change in attitudes and beliefs has put the laborer where he/she is today. And now, we, the present, soon to be the past, can create the future.

### Discussion Questions

1. What do you feel are the student's strengths and weaknesses as a writer? How can you use these to determine your approach to revision?

2. What area of the paper will you focus on during this session? Will you suggest a revision strategy which the student might be able to use in a subsequent writing task?

3. How can the concept of audience and purpose help focus the revision?

4. Do you feel this student is comfortable incorporating outside material into his own text? Is there a crouton in this text? Can you suggest an approach to working with sources which might be helpful to this student?

You may also find it helpful to use the **Worksheet For Examining Sources in a Text,** reprinted on the following page.

## Essays About Literature

Two common assignments students bring to the writing center are those of the book review and the literary essay. Both types of assignments cause problems for students, partly because they may be unfamiliar with strategies for analyzing literature but also because they may not understand the nature of the tasks they are being asked to fulfill. Of course, the requirements of these two genres are too complex to address adequately here; however, I would like you to be aware of some typical difficulties students encounter.

### The Book Review

The book review is a particularly confusing assignment because the models students see in newspapers and magazine often contain a great deal of plot summary, when, in actuality, the aim of the academic book review essay is to

# WORKSHEET FOR EXAMINING SOURCES IN A TEXT*

1. What types of source material are used in this paper (journal articles, encyclopedias, books, etc.)

2. Where is the source material located (primarily in one or two sections or dispersed and integrated in the argument?)

3. How is the source material incorporated into this paper? (paraphrased? summarized briefly or at some length? densely synthesized, material from several sources "stacked?" quoted? given a reference only?) Are there croutons in this text?

4. What context/introduction is provided for each type of source material? (none, the writer's name only? name and identity? explanation of the context of the previous work?)

5. What is the function of the references? (as proof/evidence? to support a position or interpretation? to establish authority? to contradict another position?)

*Based on Margaret R. Kirkland, *Intertextuality in Discourse Community Culture: An Analytical Tool. Conference on College Composition and Communication* convince an intelligent readership that a particular book is or is not worth read-ing—that is, the review should have an argumentative thrust. Because students do not understand this, they often write plot summaries instead of developing a thesis about the book supported with evidence from the text. In helping students write book reviews, then, find out if the student really understands what the as-signment requires. Point out that some form of plot summary should be included in order to give the reader a sense of what the book is about, but that the pri-mary purpose of the review, usually, is to convince an audience that the book is or is not valuable in some way. Here are some questions you might find useful:

1. Are the characters believable? Are they well developed?
2. Does the plot keep your attention? How does it do so?
3. Does the book raise important questions about our society? About relation-ships?
4. Is it well-written? How would you characterize the author's style? Is it de-scriptive? Evocative?
5. Does the book address an important controversy? Does it take an unusual position?

In responding to these questions, students should find examples in the text that illustrate their ideas. They can use the Note Synthesis Sheet to record quotations they might wish to use.

## The Essay About a Work of Literature

Students have difficulty writing about works of literature for the same rea-son they do when they are assigned to write book reviews—they often don't un-derstand what sort of essay they are supposed to write and therefore simply write a plot summary. In working with students on these types of assignments, then, you should emphasize that the essay about literature aims to persuade readers of an idea or point concerning the particular literary work and that they will be using evidence from the text and sometimes the opinions of others to support their views. Point out that there must be a definable focused thesis that ties together all the specific claims made in the paper. A. M. and Charlene Tib-betts (*Strategies of Rhetoric with Handbook.* Fifth edition. Glenview, Illinois: Scott, Foresman and Company, 1987) suggest that students should think of themselves as writing for an audience who has read the work but may not have thought of the idea that the writer is presenting. They sum up the writer's relationship with their reader as follows:

I have read a work (that you also have read), and I have an idea about it that may have not occurred to you. I am going to explain this idea, giving you examples from the work to prove my point, and I hope when I am through that you will agree with me (449).

## Helping Students Understand a Literary Work

When students come to the writing center with an assignment to write about a work of literature, you can help them understand the work by asking them the following questions:

1. **What happens in the work?** Ask students to summarize the plot and tell you about the characters. Ask them which character they think is the main character and whether that character faces any conflict. Perhaps that conflict is physical; more often it is psychological or emotional. Ask students if they can find the climax or turning point within the story or if there is a point where loose threads are tied together or when a decision is made.

2. **What is the "theme" of the work? Or what does the work say?** Point out that many writers of poetry, drama, and fiction have ideas about society or about human relationships and that works of literature often raise issues or themes for the reader to consider. Some works of literature clearly emphasize a particular idea, and the author's idea of right and wrong are clearly presented, perhaps even one-sided. But others often show that human nature and human decision making is complex and that it is difficult to determine absolute right and wrong. In fact, most important works of literature do not have clearly defined heroes and villains, and concepts of right and wrong are presented as complex.

3. **Does the author have a clear voice in this work?** Ask students if they can trace a narrative voice that tells a story or if they can determine the author's point of view. Sometimes works of fiction are presented from a first person viewpoint, in which case, the writer functions almost as a character within the story. At other times, the writer assumes an omniscient viewpoint, in which case he or she can present thoughts and feelings of all characters and summarize all actions which pertain to the story. Sometimes the author attempts to be completely objective in the telling of the story and presents "facts" without authorial comment.

4. **Where is the author physically, socially and temporally located in this work?** Often, the narrator stands outside the narration—he or she is simply an observer of the events being related. This distance may be the result of actual physical or social separation (the narrator is an outsider, as in *Gulliver's Travels*) or because the narrator is telling about something that happened a long time ago, in which case, time has created the narrator's distance from the narrated events. Asking students about the location of the narrator to events being narrated or described is also helpful when helping

students to analyze a poem. Since many poets write about particular scenes or landscapes, it is helpful to ask students if they can see the poet and view what is being described through his or her eyes. This can help the student understand the perspective of the work.

5. **How is the work organized? What is the structure of the work?** Ask students how the literary work is shaped or how it gets its form. If it is a play, does it have scenes and acts? If so, how do these divisions create the shape of the story? If it is a fictional work, is it divided into chapters or episodes? Do different sections deal with different perspectives? If it is a poem, is there a pattern of stanzas or sections? Can the student locate any repetition or patterns within the work?

6. **Are there problems in the work? Is the work unsuccessful in some way?** This question is very helpful in enabling students to think of ideas, since they can focus their papers in exploring where the work may not have succeeded. Is a character poorly developed? Are the characters too "black and white," or unbelievable? Is the action improbable? Is the tone too uneven (too hysterical or too flat)? Is the value system completely dated? Questions such as these can help students clarify for themselves their overall reaction to the work and can enable them to think about a possible thesis.

## Finding "Evidence" for the Literary Paper

Another reason that students encounter difficulties in writing about literature is that they may not know how to provide evidence for the claims they make. They assert something, refer briefly to the plot and assume that they have proven a case. Therefore, one important way that writing center tutors can help students with literary papers is to teach them how to take notes from or mark a text in order to gather evidence for their essays. Suggest that students read the text more than once, the first time to get a sense of its major themes and structure, the second with the aim of seeking out puzzles or anomalies, to mark passages that confuse them or contradict what they previously believed the work to be about. Have them question the actions of the characters (why do they do the things they do? What do they notice about the narrator?) Assure students that few literary critics read a work only once, and that they will perceive the text with greater complexity if they read it several times, gathering "evidence" for the points they wish to make. The Source Note Sheets and the Note Synthesis Sheets discussed above can also be useful for gathering this type of evidence. Learning to incorporate quotations into the text also pertains to assignments concerned with literature.

## Other Problems with the Literary Essay

In addition to writing plot summaries and not knowing how to gather evidence, students often attempt to cover too many possibilities—characters, settings, plots, symbols, themes—everything they can think of. Urge students to narrow their focus—perhaps to concentrate on the effect of a particular character on the plot, to trace a change in a character, to examine the role of the setting on a character's decision, or to find patterns of imagery that help the story to unfold or which provide a counterpoint to the apparent mood of the story. Another common misunderstanding is that there must be one "right" interpretation to a literary work, as if it is a puzzle that must be solved. Students should aim for an interpretation which they can support with evidence, one which is not simply a matter of opinion.

The discussions that take place in the writing center about literature are, unto themselves, extremely useful in enabling students to understand works of literature. Even if the tutor has not read the work (and no tutor can have read every work a student may be assigned), the above questions can generate a great deal of enlightenment. Actually, after you work with several students on the same work of literature, you will feel as if you have already read it, even if you hadn't previously!

## For Further Exploration

Writing about literature is a study unto itself about which a great deal has been written. Here is a list of some additional sources which you might find helpful:

Minot, Stephen. *Reading Fiction.* Englewood Cliffs, New Jersey: Prentice-Hall, 1985.

Perrine, Laurence. *Sound and Sense: An Introduction to Literature.* Find rest Petrosky, Anthony R. "From Story to Essay: Reading and Writing." *College Composition and Communications.* 23 (1982): 19–36.

Rosenblatt, Louise. *Literature as Exploration.* New York: Noble, 1965.

Suleiman, Susan R. and Inge Crosman, Eds. *The Reader in the Text: Essays on Audience and Interpretation.* Princeton: Princeton University Press, 1980.

Tomkins, Jane P. Ed. *Reader-Response Criticism: From Formalism to Post-Structuralism.* Baltimore: The Johns Hopkins University Press, 1980.

# *Writing Center Resources*

The *Writing Center Journal* publishes substantive articles concerned with issues pertaining to writing centers. It includes a yearly bibliography of relevant publications.

*Writing Center Journal*
Nance Grimm
Department of Humanities
Michigan Technological University
Houghton, Michigan 49931

The *Writing Lab Newsletter* contains many helpful suggestions for working in the writing center. It also serves as a vehicle for announcing national and regional conferences, local meetings, potential research projects, and requests for information.

*Writing Lab Newsletter*
Muriel Harris, Editor
Department of English
Purdue University
Heavilon Hall
West Lafayette, Indiana 47907

The National Writing Centers Association provides starter kits for beginning writing centers and holds sessions at two conferences: The National Council of Teachers of English (NCTE) conference in November and the Conference on College Composition and Communication (CCCC) held in March. The organization also has regional divisions. Since a new president is chosen every year for the NWCA, it is best to consult the *Writing Lab Newsletter* for membership information.

## Books Concerned with Writing Centers

Many of these contain useful bibliographies

Arkin, Marian. *Tutoring ESL Students: A Guide For Tutors (And Teachers) in the Subject Areas.* New York: Longman, 1982.

Arkin, Marian, and Barbara Shollar. *The Tutor Book.* New York: Longman, 1982.

Clark, Beverly Lyon. *Talking ABout Writing: A Guide for Tutor and Teacher Conferences.* Ann Arbor, Michigan: University of Michigan Press, 1988.

Farrell, Pamela. *The High School Writing Center: Establishing and Maintaining One.* Urbana: NCTE, 1990.

Freedman, Sarah W. et al. *The Role of Response in the Acquisition of Written Language.* Final Report to the National Institute of Education, 1985.

Harris, Muriel, Ed. *Tutoring Writing: A Sourcebook for Writing Labs.* Glenview, Illinois: Scott Foresman, 1982.

———. Teaching One-to-One: The Writing Conference. Urbana, NCTE, 1986.

Maxwell, Martha, ed. *When Tutor Meets Student: Experiences in Collaborative Learning.* Kensington, MD: MM Associates, 1990.

Meyer, Emily, and Louise Z. Smith. *The Practical Tutor.* New York: Oxford University Press, 1987.

Olson, Gary A. *Writing Centers: Theory and Administration.* Urbana: NCTE, 1984.

Reigstad, Thomas J. and Donald A. McAndrew. *Training Tutors for Writing Conferences: Theory and Research into Practice.* Urbana, Illinois: Educational Resources Information Center and National Council of Teachers of English, 1984.

Schiff, Peter. *The Teacher-Student Writing Conference: New Approaches.* Urbana: ERIC Clearing House on Reading and Communication Skills, 1978.

Stewart, Joyce S. and Mary K. Croft. *The Writing Laboratory: Organization, Management, and Methods.* Glenview, Illinois: Scott Foresman, 1982.

Wallace, Ray, and Jeanne Simpson, Eds. *The Writing Center: New Directions.* New York: Garland Publishing Inc.: 1991.

# INDEX